Dyslexics Are *Orchids,*

• • • • • • • •

Mothers Are *Gardeners*

Dyslexics Are *Orchids,*

· · · · · · · · ·

Mothers Are *Gardeners*

James Arthur O'Leary, M.D.
and Cindy Jayne Brewer

Published by Open Pages Publishing, LLC
Estero, Florida

Dyslexics Are Orchids, Mothers Are Gardeners

James O'Leary

copyright © 2019

ISBN: 978-1-7322722-1-7 (sc)
ISBN: 978-1-7322722-2-4 (eBook)
Library of Congress Control Number: 2019912826

Printed and bound in the United States of America.

Disclaimer
The information in this book is:
- of a general nature and not intended to address the specific circumstances of a particular individual or entity;
- not gender specific; you will find instances where "he/him/his" is mentioned but it can also refer to "she/her";
- written as a guide and is not intended to be a comprehensive tool, but is complete, accurate, or up to date at the time of writing;
- an information tool only and not intended to be used in place of a visit, consultation, or advice of a medical, legal or other type of professional.

Original logo/cover design by Christine Dupre
Interior design by Juanita Dix and Amy Dangler
Published by Open Pages Publishing, LLC – http://openpagespublishing.com

Your Pathways
· · · · · · · · · · ·

Dedication

* * * * * * * * * *

Mom, Gladys Estelle Arthur O'Leary, 1905-1946,
Dad, James Leonard O'Leary, MD, 1905–1974,
and to all mothers caring for their dyslexic child.

Dear Mom,

I love you and cherish you beyond words. You made my life worth living. Without you I would not have survived.

You really "got it" and understood me. You showed me the patience I needed. You put your life and career on hold to help me.

You taught me everything I needed to know; how to problem solve, be organized, deal with bullies and create a plan. You helped me on my down days when I was frustrated, angry or depressed. Even my social skill deficits succumbed to your love and patience.

I am grateful for your persistence, your determination, your sacrifices and most of all for your love. You taught me how to be a friend by caring and showing gratitude to those I love.

Mom, you were the "bestest" mom on earth and truly a gift from God. Your comfort and love helped me through my darkest days.

Thank you for your love and compassion.

Acknowledgement

Some authors are fortunate to have many people as advisors, assistants, associates, supporters, observers and professionals who provide help.

I have been blessed to have a few good friends and family who have given me the strength and the impetus to continue to persist, and stay determined despite many potholes and speed bumps over the past 12 months. I am forever grateful to:

Cynthia Vander Wielen, Consultant, Advisor, and Friend
Elizabeth Ann O'Leary
James Leonard O'Leary, II, Esq.
April Christina O'Leary, Daughter by Marriage
Amy Fox Dangler, no words exist to describe her many contributions, a friend.
Cindy Jayne Brewer, Friend, Formatter and Editor

This book would never exist without their input, understanding and kindness.

Reflections

. . . .

This book is a reflection of life experiences working with mothers who are dealing with dyslexia. Through all of his professional career experiences, the most important fact that he has learned is that a child with dyslexia can be happy and successful!

Parenting a child in today's world is tough enough, but add in dyslexia and a recipe is created with emotional and physical exhaustion for mothers. It is likely the hardest thing a mom will have to do in her whole life. From watching your child struggle in the classroom, to working with administrators and tutors, realizing the root cause, and finally helping your child conquer and deal with dyslexia as a mom can feel like an uphill battle in every way.

But here lies the HOPE - from experience he has observed and learned that the number one factor in a child's success is a stable, **understanding** and loving home. Knowing this far exceeds any other contributing issues. It is very important that you recognize other problems, issues or disorders in your child as early as possible, i.e., anxiety, depression, frustration, ADD, and especially social and emotional difficulties. He has observed that the presence of any other issue will dramatically reduce your success and may lead to frustration and failure.

While reading this book, you may have the feeling that someone has been with you in the home during your times of struggle and had seen the fits of anger, the depression, the tears, fear and exhaustion which seem constant companions in the struggle to **understand** and help your child.

In a very real way Dr. O'Leary has a unique and valuable point of view because he writes as both a dyslexic person with Asperger's and has experienced the confusion of growing up in a world that **understood** nothing about dyslexia. As a physician, father and grandfather, he has continued to seek out answers to help those who are still struggling today to find HOPE in the diagnosis and challenges of dyslexia.

Dr. O'Leary will acknowledge and affirm your emotions, as well as those of your daughter or son. He will share his life experiences and those of mothers caring for their dyslexic child.

In the fall of 2015, he began volunteering to help students and mothers struggling with problems stemming from dyslexia. The work and research he began grew into the chapters that follow.

He will place great importance on the roles of HOPE, **understanding**, patience, kindness and love.

HOPE will help you **understand**, and **understanding** will give you HOPE.

Author's Experience

As a young child, I knew I was different. I didn't understand why my friends could read and I had great difficulty. I felt very alone and thought I was stupid. My family tried to help, but they had no idea what was going on with me. They thought I was just "slow."

I failed to fit in, so instead I became the "tag-along" or totally isolated. Overwhelming feelings of dependency and fear were my constant companions. I longed just to be "normal."

Emotionally, I was a mess. I felt isolated because in my mind I was "different." I was fearful that classmates would find out my weaknesses and not like me. I thought my only choice to survive was to become the "invisible student." No one would see that I couldn't read and that I didn't know the first thing about the lesson being taught. Always sitting in the last row, I kept my head down and made believe I was reading. I never made eye contact.

My biggest fear was being asked to read out loud. I would do anything not to have to read in front of the class and show everyone the embarrassing truth. I would hem and haw, pause, guess, mispronounce, stutter and stumble. I would try to just reach the end of the passage without too many mistakes.

But as hard as I tried to pretend, I could tell that the teachers and other kids knew I had problems reading.

I hated how embarrassed I was, but I hated even more that the teachers and my classmates were embarrassed for me.

• •

After I finished my turn reading aloud, I couldn't look at any-body. I just wanted to crawl under my desk and hide. Merci-fully, the teacher would not usually ask me to read out loud a second time. My best subject was recess and going home.

Your Child...

I come to school to read and write
just like all the other children.
But I can't. I'm on my own.

Reading is a maze of letters.
Writing makes my head hurt.

My refuge is my room.
I sit on my bed and cry.
What should be easy is hard for me.

ABOUT THE AUTHOR

. . . .

James A. O'Leary, M.D.
Is a graduate of Georgetown University Medical School and spent his career working with mothers with high-risk pregnancies for four decades. He authored the only book to date on birth injuries, *Shoulder Dystocia and Birth Injuries*. He was a tenured professor at Loyola University and The State University of New York. Having published 200 peer-reviewed medical articles, he is an expert in not only research and education, he too struggles with dyslexia. He is a grandfather to three girls and volunteers extensively at a school for dyslexic children in Naples, FL. He and his wife Arlene reside in Naples and he enjoys spending his free time reading and enjoying his family.

Cindy Jayne Brewer
I am first and most importantly, a mom of a dyslexic daughter who amazes me everyday with her wit, intelligence, talent and tenacity. I home-schooled my two children for five years and educated myself on dyslexia by reading, researching and attending seminars on the subject. I later taught at a school for dyslexic students and am currently an educator at a local high school where I teach drama, music and speech. I have a BA from Samford University and plan to pursue my masters in Education.

I have run the gamete of all the emotions discussed in this book—from sadness and confusion, frustration and depression to acceptance and understanding. Being a part of this book has been both therapeutic and encouraging. I hope that every mom who picks up this book will feel the same comfort, camaraderie and most importantly, the HOPE that I have.

UNDERSTANDING DYSLEXIA

"A mother understands what a child does not say."
- Jewish Proverb

A MOTHER'S REALITY

Feelings are not always facts and thoughts are the seeds of change. If you correct your thoughts your feelings will follow. Never forget **HOPE** is omnipotent.

- Moms are a large part of a child's success. Actually, the greatest part!

- A mom's life is very hard in almost every way possible. Raising a child with dyslexia is the single greatest obstacle a mother will ever experience. **HOPE** and **understanding** will help you get through life.

- Remember that reading is not the only problem, there is a lot more to it.

 Behind every child who believes in himself
is a parent who believed first.

• •

A MOTHER'S JOURNEY

It is critical for you to have a network of friends and family around you who know, understand and support you. Their knowledge of dyslexia and empathy can fill the holes that you just CAN'T. This is because you do not yet know the "potholes and speed bumps" that will come your way.

> An enduring catalyst will be the tears in your child's eyes as they try to understand why they can't read. Your child needs answers and the understanding, which comes from compassion.

This is a story that I love of how one mother dealt with her child:

I am a wife, a mother and a dyslexia warrior. My only child, a daughter who was diagnosed with dyslexia and dysgraphia at the age of seven, taught me the importance of fighting. It was then that I embraced this journey for all it was worth. I know that my child needs me to stand up for her and be her voice. She needs me to make sure I fight for her legal rights at all costs.

This author feels compelled to bring her story, because she believes it is important to find someone who can share an ever-increasing knowledge to help anyone who finds themselves on this journey. No mother needs to feel alone.

www. amomsjourney-mydyslexiclife.com

> Anger is a frequent ongoing problem in those who care for someone with dyslexia. It is always hovering below the surface. Emotional issues usually occur out of frustration in social situations, dealing with school issues or at home. I have observed that frustration frequently produces depression and anger.

It is also common for children with dyslexia to release their anger on parents. Mothers are more likely to feel their wrath.

During adolescence children are expected to become mature. Frequently, just the opposite occurs. Moms need to know that this is a very real possibility.

Adolescence for a child with dyslexia is a much different experience than a regular child because of their social weaknesses. I recommend that you keep this in mind. It will help you understand and prepare for the process.

Childhood conflicts are caused by the tension between wanting to free and yet still need to be dependent. Your child's anger is used to break away from the people on whom they feel so dependent, even you. Be ready to not take what could appear as negative or hurtful, personally. Learning to keep your cool will help you to become a much "cooler" parent.

Remember, a child with dyslexia has a sense of being trapped and unable to perform properly. Their frustration can turn into depression, then anger. This frustration is frequently a daily experience and has a specific target: parent, teacher, adult or sibling who is perceived as thwarting their needs. Be prepared to understand with love.

 I never knew how much love my heart could hold –
Until someone called me Mommy.

UNDERSTANDING DYSLEXIA

My experience has taught me that most moms need to understand how to compensate in one way or another with all of their child's personal issues. I call them "work-arounds" (Page 163). Others call them accommodations. Often, your child may compensate by becoming an invisible student, but it is essential to also compensate by working hard on their strengths. It is critical for your child to **understand and know their own interests and strengths**.

• •

In my personal experience **understanding** is essential, a key foundation issue and very helpful. As I see it, this **understanding** is an important building block that will help you and your child develop HOPE. HOPE can lead to **understanding** and **understanding** leads to **HOPE**.

Sometimes, your child may simply shut down. They may decide not to try and learn anymore. This shutting down may even lead to dropping out of school entirely. Understand that your child is very sensitive, vulnerable and struggles with feelings of frustration, regret and rejection. Dyslexics are hyper-emotional and do not handle rejection very well.

Unfortunately, your child with dyslexia may feel that the way to express their fear of embarrassment is with anger. If the anger is directed inward, they can become depressed. If directed outward, it may become rage and acting out. Both parents and children may be totally unaware of this process. If the adults in their lives can discern what is happening, the child will have a much better chance of **understanding** their emotions and reactions, and work on other, better ways to express themselves.

Be cognizant that a child may think that if they act as though "school is stupid," no one will see their fear and feelings of self-loathing. The danger is that some children may drop out, get into drugs or wind up joining a gang to deal with their feelings of loneliness and isolation.

A mother of a middle school student said to me, *"You should know that your child will try to cover up their fear of discovery and feelings of inferiority. This is due to anxiety and poor reading skills, which leads to an inability to succeed in school. In most cases, the children are simply crying out for help. They very often hide their feelings and don't know how to express these emotions."*

> You will need to protect your child's rights to learn differently and she needs to be allowed to thrive as herself, so she can be the best she can possibly imagine.

Your child is like a butterfly in the wind.
Some can fly higher than others,
But each one flies the best it can.
Why compare one against the other?
Each one is different.
Each one is special.
Each one is beautiful.

—Lessonslearnedinlife.com

I have noticed that as education progresses into middle school, high school and college, many different emotional pressures and demands arise.

An awareness begins to grow that dyslexia affects more than reading and writing, and that it can impinge every aspect of a person's life and have a devastating and long-term effect on self-esteem and cause scarring in the brain.

In particular, college seems to be a place that demands **understanding** in some ways while intentionally ignoring it in other ways. Frequently, nothing is done about the sense of isolation, because schools and teachers are unaware of the multifaceted dimensions of dyslexia – different ways of processing information, dealing with dyslexia anger, misunderstandings, and both internal and external judgments made by those teaching and learning. Parents should be ready to become a strong advocate.

> True Story
> Children learn more from WHO YOU ARE than what you teach.

It is very apparent to me that some mothers may not be experienced in dealing with their own emotional repercussions of dyslexia. They may not see how emotions can be presented in many convoluted ways!

The educational system needs to make non-dyslexic students aware that dyslexia is a disorder that can be dealt with successfully. Call it a connection issue. I like "a different reading style." They should be made aware of your child's needs and their different learning style.

Moms need to understand that every day their child with dyslexia must deal with poor concentration, memory lapses, emotional dysregulation and sensitivity to noise, light and texture. This goes along with their feelings of shame, embarrassment, guilt and fear of their limitations being found out. These can be overwhelming and often begin every morning right after getting out of bed. It is very much like a ticking time bomb!! Actually, difficulty getting out of bed is common. Having a routine and preparing for the next day the night before can decrease a lot of anxiety and frustration in the morning.

However, at the same time your child may be inspiringly creative, show an innate ability to problem solve, possess a vibrant visual recall and amazing artistic talents. Identifying and strongly encouraging their strengths will greatly add to the ability to balance the difficulties of dyslexia with their unique and special talents.

God could not be everywhere, and therefore, He made Mothers!
— Rudyard Kipling

Being dyslexic is like being on a seesaw of ability and disability, never quite knowing when a mind full of ideas will disintegrate into a mind full of blankness and confusion.

It is no surprise that many children and adults will suffer from an unrelenting generalized anxiety and depression that can escalate to full-blown Post-Traumatic Stress Disorder. This can trigger adverse emotional coping strategies and can scar your child's mind with long-term effort.

There is HOPE if these issues are recognized and dealt with in an understanding and loving way. There is a need for parents, family, educators and counsellors to consider the emotional vulnerabilities of dyslexia.

I believe dyslexia is inextricably woven into self-image, self-confidence and self-esteem. This "lacking" impacts everyone – not just the child, but the whole family. However, it is much worse for the child, especially in school.

 I want to re-emphasize: mothers please understand that your child was born this way. They don't like it either. They just came this way. Your child with dyslexia is trying to make sense of where they belong and hoping their efforts are respected and accepted.

Your child needs to learn how to deal with other people who either don't think or act the same way as they do. You need to keep this in mind as you and your child grow together. Being prepared in advance is extremely important. Always have a plan A, B and C!

Many dyslexic children may also have ADD (Attention Deficit Disorder) and a mild form of high functioning autistic spectrum disorder called Asperger's Syndrome. Social anxiety is a constant companion.

The term "autistic spectrum" disorder seems to create a pejorative feeling, while the word Asperger's is more acceptable. In my personal experience, very few people know about Asperger's and seem not to care; whereas autism is a serious stigma. Social and emotional education can be very effective in creating an understanding and kind environment at school and at home.

> With no teacher training on dyslexia awareness, school can be a minefield for both mothers seeking access to the right support and teachers being challenged to find a way for students to learn.

I want to repeat that the ravages of multiple emotional turmoil may ultimately force you to seek help from a counsellor or tutors. With no training in dyslexia awareness, teachers may not appreciate what "being dyslexic" means.

They do not realize the complicated emotional landscape that can be expressed through adverse emotional coping strategies. Mothers especially should be on guard. The problem is that the one thing moms need the most of, is TIME and this is the one thing they have the least.

Understand:
- Dyslexia is a many faceted disorder that is often not appreciated.
- It can be seen within a spectrum from mild to severe, which can make it difficult to deal with.

- It will vary from day to day.
- Identify and recognize strengths so they can be incorporated into home life which will help deal with weaknesses.
- The degree of impact will vary according to what children are trying to do and its difficulty.
- Needs should be addressed on an individual basis.

Mom, is this forever?

Dyslexia can resemble a "stew or Bolognese sauce or a smorgasbord," metaphorically speaking. And you are in charge of the "kitchen."

One of the best representations of dyslexia is an iceberg. The majority lies beneath the surface. In dyslexia, the reading difficulty aspect is just the tip of the iceberg.

There frequently may be many other serious issues just below the surface – *ADD, social anxiety, depression, OCD and sensory disorders* to name a few, which can be dealt with if only when they are properly recognized.

Every child with dyslexia is unique and does not resemble any other child with dyslexia, but there can be some overlay. Some of their brain connections may be different, not abnormal connections, which require a "different learning style."

Dyslexia is and always will be a part of who your child is. If he or she can appreciate what the causation is, their ability to succeed is improved.

Dyslexia is challenging to **understand**. I have personally observed this. It affects emotions, social connections, friendships, family relationships and all aspects of life. It can be overwhelming.

Creating an internal monologue helps to affirm that one's best is enough, things *will* get better, happiness *is* attainable and that success is there, right around the corner. This will go a long way in keeping **HOPE** alive in both parent and child.

A child with dyslexia may be slow and some days even slower, but once they feel **understood**, they have a tenaciousness that often far exceeds the "normal" child.

Even though they may experience hurtful feedback from those who don't **understand** the challenges of dyslexia, they will only grow stronger and more determined to prove that they can and will learn!

When parents remain strong advocates and join together with their child in this journey, there really is nothing that can't be accomplished.

There are NO single solutions. There are many fads designed to take your money and are not proven to be successful.

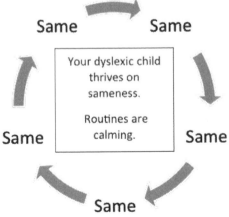

Same   Same

Your dyslexic child
thrives on
sameness.

Routines are
calming.

Same   Same

Same

Maternal Experience:

I have frequently interacted with moms who blame themselves because of an apparent delay in diagnosis. They lament and wish they could have provided earlier intervention. Knowing that guilt is common can ease the fear and anxiety many mothers feel. Frequently mothers also wonder if they did something wrong during the pregnancy. *No way.* Dyslexia is genetic!

This is illustrated by a friend and mother who stated that:
"I feel sad, because I noticed this too late...I see other children were sent to this teaching center at the age of five to six years old, which is earlier than my son...I sent my son only when he was in elementary school...If only I realized it earlier."

> For many children, dyslexia is recognized later in school only because their progress is slow.

ARE WE ALL THE SAME?
Mommy, am I different?

There are several reasons that parents should consider this question. The first and most obvious is the implications for parenting, teaching, and social and emotional life skills.

If distinct subtypes within dyslexia were recognizable, different types of teaching and intervention might be useful to meet these needs. Unfortunately, this is NOT true. If you know a dyslexic, you still don't know dyslexia. I see this every time I interact with children at our local dyslexia school or in after-school activities.

All children with dyslexia have different strengths! Our brains have 100 billion to 200 billion nerves. These can take years to fully develop, usually by age 23. Add this to the many connections each single nerve possesses. This can lead to a possible total of 76 trillion connections, and our 3 to 3½ pound brains come in many variations.

Therefore, I want to repeat that a child's learning and reading style will also be different and highly variable. There's the key word – variable. Dyslexia is a beautiful variation, not a disability.

Understanding that dyslexia is a connection issue and not a disease will bring HOPE and encouragement.

> Every one of us is different,
> but we still have much in common.

In my opinion, this needs to be re-emphasized ...mothers should be forgiven for thinking that many dyslexics have pretty much the same connection impairments. The fact is, it's simply not true. Every dyslexic is special and unique, but also very hypersensitive, vulnerable and susceptible to rejection and criticism.

Fellow dyslexics can recognize and **understand** each other. Often, having a friend who is also dyslexic can help a child to feel less alone and more accepted. If dyslexics had only one specific connection issue, this would raise concerns because of the many emotional factors interacting with dyslexia.

Other Factors of Dyslexia Include:
- Other cognitive skills; math, spelling, reading, sounding out words
- Early language experience
- Learning style
- Short term memory
- Personality
- Formal teaching of reading
- Developmental state
- Compensatory strategies
- Social experiences
- Etc., etc., etc....

The differences in brain connectivity can be seen in certain issues that often display themselves, such as the confusion between left and right, putting shoes on opposite feet and quirky eating habits. These are called Sensory Processing Disorders. But are these issues really that important? What is needed is to identify what is important!

Developing "work-arounds" can help to de-stress many situations that could cause high anxiety. For example, if left and right cause confusion, one could use a small tape on the arm which corresponds with the directional word.

If the challenge involves shoes, label the child's socks with an L and R and draw an L and R with a Sharpie on the bottom of the corresponding shoe.

Every child and adult living with, or helping someone with dyslexia will eventually develop many helpful "work-arounds" for everyday life. Some children may do this to get attention. Many of these issues gradually resolve. I like to say this too will pass.

How Moms can help their child to embrace the power of dyslexia:

♥ Believe in yourself. Dyslexia teaches you to budget your time and work hard. This work ethic will help no matter what you decide to do in life. It isn't easy, but it is simple!

♥ Talk to others who are dyslexic and listen to their success stories! They will inspire and encourage you. If they did it, you can, too!

❤ Remember that just because something takes you longer to do, doesn't mean you can't do it well. And sometimes, because it takes longer, you remember it better.

❤ They may feel different or singled out. If your child needs extra help or tutoring, try to remember that they're learning the skills to overcome dyslexia—and that they are smart and have abilities no one else does!

❤ Identify and embrace their strengths. Children with dyslexia may be perceived as being at risk for failure academically, socially and emotionally. This may sound repetitive, but is the key to the success of your child. Self-awareness and self-acceptance can be learned if they are aware of themselves.

Understanding that they may have to teach others how to **understand** them will encourage self-honesty and emotional maturity. Remember mom, you are the teacher and the gardener.

Difficulties in learning may lead to social and behavioral issues in school, at home or life in general.

> Tip:
> Always anticipate problems and have a plan A, B and even C.
> Remember, failing to plan is planning to fail.

Expecting others not to **understand** can prepare the child for future **misunderstandings** that may occur.

It is very important that mothers not lose **HOPE** and realize that dyslexia is not a diagnosis of failure. Children will pick up on any negative feelings and will internalize a mother's fears as something wrong with themselves. Remember: **HOPE** is everything!

The stress and insecurity your child feels can cause all sorts of problems for moms. When dyslexics have to deal with people who don't understand the emotional and social issues, they may experience fear and use strategies of avoidance and self-blaming.

Mothers need to sit down, talk with their child and explain how to deal with possible negative or confusing reactions. This will probably be an ongoing process.

> Children with dyslexia are all very sensitive and vulnerable, especially to rejection.
> Rejection can be destructive!

Your child can suffer from rejection from family members, parents, grandparents, teachers or friends. The loss of a meaningful relationship can be very serious. Some children may develop PTSD (post-traumatic stress disorder), a brain-scarring event.

It's very possible that children will experience feelings of shame, failure, inadequacy, low self-esteem, HOPElessness and helplessness.

As one child explained it, "I don't understand. I always try to be so nice to everyone at school, but a lot of the kids look at me weird because I am kind.

Even my best friend left me once we went to middle school. Instead of sticking by me, it was more important for her to be popular and I wasn't willing to be mean in order to be popular. I still miss her. I don't know if I'll ever get over being dumped by her!"

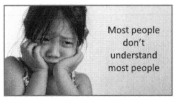

Most people don't understand most people

This rejection will be internalized and become very injuring and may result in brain scarring. But having a safe place of love and compassion where she can be herself, makes all the difference in the world – especially the world of a dyslexic child.

Be on Guard:

- For a child with dyslexia the end of a genuine friendship may cause emotional issues that can lead to PTSD, depression and a scarred mind.

- At school, your child may be seen as slow or perceived as "lazy" and not trying hard enough. Their failures may be interpreted as bad behavior or a bad attitude. This **misunderstanding** can cause the teacher to become impatient and blame the child.

  This only increases anxiety, frustration and confusion. **Understanding** themselves and knowing that mom is nearby, ready to offer additional **understanding**, can bring much comfort.

- Mothers must prepare themselves and their child to anticipate the unexpected.

- Children with dyslexia will very often be looked at as having low self-esteem and negative self-perception. This is not true.

Parents and teachers should not perceive reduced academic success as a single issue. Parents must address the social and emotional problems associated with dyslexia at school. These problems need to be addressed in conjunction with specific educational objectives.

When this is done, both children and mothers will have a better chance of coping effectively with what is a stress-inducing solvable problem. Dyslexia must be well **under-**

stood at school as part of a complex issue, as well as a unique learning style!

Dyslexics...

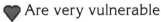 Are very vulnerable

 Find rejection an overwhelming experience, which can frequently require professional help. Remember, intense, negative emotion can persist for years.

A Mother's Personal Experience:

I can see and have seen that mothers can feel very sad, guilt ridden and disappointed when they expect to have a "normal" child, but learn their child has dyslexia. I share their tears. In addition, mothers can often feel depressed when they receive complaints from teachers that their child is slower in reading and writing compared to other students of the same age.

During an interview session, one mother was crying when she described:

"I felt down when one of the tutoring teachers told me that my son has no future and cannot be successful in his life...that he will not perform well in his future career...and that he can only work at fast-food restaurants ...[crying]...when I think about this, I feel very sad."

CHALLENGES

Most moms are working mothers who work long and exhausting hours, both at home and/or outside the home. There is little time for friendships to be made or kept up, and even maintaining a friendly acquaintance can be a struggle.

Children with dyslexia require a lot of extra time because they need help with the many learning challenges, intrinsic in their diagnosis – not just reading, writing and math, but the additional time required to first understand the homework themselves!

The extra care and attention necessary can unintentionally hurt relationships within the family.

This may result in marital discord and sibling rivalry. Even grandparents, who usually are the ones depended on to have patience with their grandchildren, can have a lack of **understanding**.

Generally, the responsibility to educate themselves about their child's learning challenges falls to the mothers. So, if they find that there is just not enough time in the day to do this, or that they don't seem to be having much success on their own, moms may have to find other solutions.

They may need to alter their daily schedule, ask a spouse to assist or even change careers. It's a never-ending daily process.

Many things end up being excluded in order to survive. Unfortunately, friends and friendships are often the first to disappear.

Forget all the reasons why it won't work and believe the one reason why it will.
—Zig Ziglar

In spite of the urgency and willingness to assist their children, moms may have a lack of knowledge about dyslexia. Some mothers may have just become aware of their child's diagnosis and have no experience from which to draw. However, all moms, no matter where they are in the journey, need extra help.

One of the main issues often stems from a **misunderstanding** that dyslexics can have significant additional challenges and thus, unknowingly moms are not able to provide the specific and appropriate support needed.

• •

Increasing financial demands are a common problem. It cannot be denied that the cost of living is rising from year to year. Many mothers are unable to find the additional time needed, because of the necessity to *continue* working as financial issues *continue* to rise.

Homelife can frequently become emotionally charged. Anger and frustration are common. Both parents and siblings need to be taught how to be patient and show understanding.

Negative feelings such as sadness, denial, worry and many others can be daily experiences for mothers who have children with dyslexia. And these often increase as the child gets older.

Denial may be one of the strategies used by moms to cope with an unacceptable reality. One of the reasons for this is because of unrealistic expectations and the opinions of others. A good lesson for us all is how to let go of what doesn't matter.

The negative feelings that affect your child will also affect mothers in their own personal and social lives. This in turn will negatively impact family life. **Mothers may need help from a health professional**, or at least from **understanding** friends and family. Counselling may eliminate or minimize negative feelings.

The good news...mothers will develop more intrinsic motivation, which will improve their own quality of life.

This can frequently be observed with mothers who connect with other mothers. Someone who has experience with dyslexia can be supportive and understanding. They will have empathy and compassion.

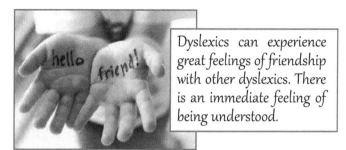

Dyslexics can experience great feelings of friendship with other dyslexics. There is an immediate feeling of being understood.

Mothers who are working outside the home still have numerous household responsibilities in addition to raising children. It seems as if the pressure to fulfill everyone's expectations can be overwhelming and unending. You must become your own advocate as well as your child's.

Mothers have no time for themselves!

Because of this, it is possible that children with dyslexia may not receive the necessary care they need and may have fewer opportunities to succeed.

Since dyslexia is a persistent condition, mothers need to be better prepared mentally and physically for the future. Support from spouses, families, friends and health professionals is rarely enough!

Too often, mothers have to carry the burden with little or no support. Only you can develop the self-awareness needed to overcome these struggles and negative emotions.

I have observed how friendship can help the mothers of a child with dyslexia. It is also very helpful if mothers get involved in a support group such as social network groups to share, exchange experiences and opinions with others who are in the same boat. Mothers *undeniably* need other people to assist them in facing the challenges of raising their dyslexic children!

Moms desperately need to experience true friendship. This is frequently overlooked.

Since many parents have a lack of knowledge about dyslexia, their frustration comes on fast and may persist.

These mothers may not know how to teach their children in the correct way. As illustrated by a mother from my group:
"We don't know how to teach him...I don't know what else I can do to help my son...I just have to tolerate whatever problems he creates."

Parents of children, who have invisible special needs often feel isolated, judged and frustrate—until they meet other parents sharing a similar journey.
—Parent to Parent of NYS/PTOPNYS.org

Dyslexia doesn't come with a manual...it comes with a parent who never gives up!!
—Amanda Kennedy

• •

REMEMBER

Mom, all of this takes strength of character,
heart, soul and mind. It takes conviction of self.
It takes resilience and determination to keep standing
strong in the face of "defeat" and repeated "nos".
All of which can be converted to "win" and "yes".
It takes love and compassion to keep going:
love for self, family, child and love and compassion for all of
those on this path. We are all facing the same challenges.
You are not alone.

EMOTIONS

· · · · · · · · · · ·

YOU MIGHT BE SAD BECAUSE
YOU'VE GONE THROUGH A
LOT, BUT YOU SHOULD ALSO BE
PROUD OF YOURSELF FOR
BEING STRONG ENOUGH TO
MAKE IT THROUGH IT.

FRUSTRATION

Your child's uniqueness requires you to be very creative in your parenting skills. Your moods can have an adverse impact on your child. Emotions in the home will have a significant effect on your child.

A common maternal worry about their children with dyslexia involves both emotional and practical difficulties. Chronic poor performance at school leads to lower self-esteem, getting frustrated and developing withdrawn or aggressive behavior.

All of these come into play when attempting to seek appropriate help, especially when things appear to move slowly in providing effective care and education to help children overcome their difficulties. This requires patience at a most difficult time.

> *Today, some mothers would say their child with dyslexia is successful by anyone's definition, but they still say that dealing with dyslexia is the single greatest obstacle in their life.*

The feelings of isolation and humiliation created even unintentionally by families can be serious obstacles. The difficulties of a dyslexic's life show the incredible impact that having dyslexia has on the family and the influence it can have on their future. Mothers almost always carry all the burden.

Mothers, by necessity, must become advocates. They may frequently be required to face school teachers who appear uncooperative and unconcerned about their child's struggle.

Dyslexia requires mothers to return repeatedly to the school to remind teachers of their child's needs and the importance of identifying problems in the classroom. It can feel like a never-ending process.

I have observed that mothers become emotionally and physically drained the more they are involved in remedial education. Moms worry about their child's future, especially marriage and job success. This will often affect the quality of sleep and contribute to a racing mind that doesn't seem to have an "off" switch.

Meditation and prayer may be helpful. Many mothers may choose to quit their jobs so they can focus all their energy and time attending to their child. As you might expect, this can create other problems, especially in the area of finances.

Remember, HOPE is omnipotent – as well as persistence and determination. Kids learn best by example. When they see mom continually fighting for and learning better ways to help them, kids will start to learn how to fight for themselves! Research reports that a large number of ongoing maternal clinical and emotional difficulties exist for mothers, because they struggle to support their child before, during and after the assessment of dyslexia. Your family's involvement is critically important.

• •

I need to reemphasize that ongoing chronic stress can lead to negative parenting practices and marital problems. It can even adversely affect the parent-child relationship.

A dyslexic's poor attachment to his/her mother is frequently due to the difficulty with schoolwork. This strains the relationships within the family.

Mothers need to be aware of this and be prepared. The amount of homework should be limited by time and **not quantity**.

Accommodations should be implemented at home and at school. After-school time is often the worst part of the day for children with dyslexia and their mothers. This is compounded by feeling tired, discouraged and overwhelmed. It is related to the maternal perception of having a relationship with a "difficult child."

A mother needs to remember that their child came this way. No one chose this. Be patient. Have **HOPE**! You are loved just as you are.

> Parental awareness of dyslexia as a lifelong disorder will empower them to guide their child from the younger years through adulthood.
>
> Ongoing support will help children learn to deal with a complex array of emotions, which are always inherent in a child with dyslexia.

Mom, your support is the protective factor that will positively impact your child's life, self-confidence and self-esteem. Mothers who support these strengths will help provide the opportunity for more positive outcomes. This is very important! The perception of support in childhood is directly related to satisfaction in adult life.

I believe the ability of parents and siblings to become a team and offer mutual support to one another will enhance feelings of being **understood and accepted**. This will bring confidence and improvements to study habits and attitude. It will very likely enhance performance as well!

Realistic parental expectations will be reflected in a child's educational expectations and academic achievements.

Wipe the tears away from your own eyes just as you have wiped them from your child's so many times before.

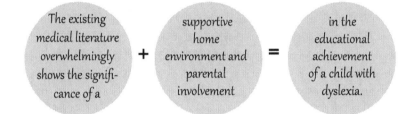

The existing medical literature overwhelmingly shows the significance of a **+** supportive home environment and parental involvement **=** in the educational achievement of a child with dyslexia.

Maternal support is what defines success

Moms are usually at the forefront of the fight to get assistance for their child. Always being a strong advocate, many mothers have to spend considerable time and resources in gaining access to:

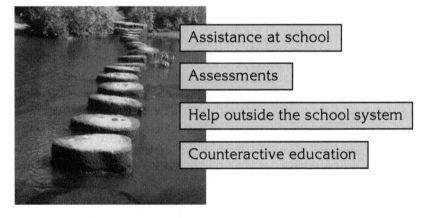

Assistance at school

Assessments

Help outside the school system

Counteractive education

• •

These stepping stones can be expensive and often beyond the financial means of many families. I suggest asking other moms for advice on how to get the necessary help in the least expensive way. Children aren't the only ones who can apply creativity and work-arounds. Moms can learn them from other mothers too!

You are so important to your kids just for being who you are.

You are more able than you believe!

Encourage yourself with the same words you use to encourage your children, "You CAN do it and it's worth it!"

A Real Mom

Emotional, yet the rock.
Tired, but keeps going.
Worried, but full of HOPE.
Impatient, yet patient.
Overwhelmed, but never quits.
Amazing, even though doubted.
Wonderful, even in the chaos.
Life changer, every single day.

—Rachel Martin

DEPRESSION

Your understanding represents the foundation for your success as a mother. Remember that dyslexics are extremely sensitive. This makes almost everything about raising your child stressful.

A very important secondary consequence of having dyslexia and raising a child with this challenge is depression. Dyslexia, and the problems it creates, bring stress for everyone involved, of which they will become increasingly aware. Such emotions can render your child very sensitized to the effects on the family and teachers.

Mothers must remain aware of these difficulties and learn how to explain things to their child in a way that helps them to understand the reactions of others, as well as easing any guilt they may feel because of their dyslexia.

Such difficulties can be manifested as confusion, frustration and even anger. Mothers can learn to become a keen and an astute observer of their child's and their own reactions.

Self-awareness and self-acceptance are critically important in maintaining your physical and emotional health.

Dealing with your child's meltdowns is hard. We all get tired, frustrated, hungry, dehydrated, lack enough sleep at times but if we recognize where we are when the storm hits, we can breathe and listen, validate until it's run its course. It's a sure sign they are overwhelmed.

In AA the word HALT is a teaching; Hungry, Angry, Lonely and Tired.

It is both the known and unknown expectations of being a successful mother which often creates problems. If you feel threatened in your ability to be a competent advocate and mother, remember stress leads to denial and denial feeds frustration which can lead to anxiety, depression and guilt.

In the absence of certain expected life experiences, your child's vulnerability and sensitivity can often result in children feeling responsibility and guilt for such situations. Remember, your child is VERY hypersensitive and vulnerable. Hints or acts of rejection are magnified and can lead to PTSD and brain scarring.

This can happen even if moms are doing all the right things. This is not something for mothers to feel guilty about.

An almost inevitable outcome for dyslexics will be the development of childhood anxiety. This will only become more intense over time and more deep-seated. High level anxiety can become a long-term problem and can be associated with external indicators such as trembling or shaking, breathing difficulties, and vocal hesitations.

These feelings can worsen with repeated exposure to criticisms and rejections. The sooner anxiety is noticed, the easier it will be to address it and lessen it with coping strategies.

> Over time, feelings can become hidden and so familiar that the person can actually come to see such a state as relatively normal. In this case, there can be an absence of external signs of anxiety, such as fear, isolation and depression.

Many children with dyslexia will show outward signs in learning and thinking styles and responses to certain activities. Sometimes, healthy changes will be observed. These are your child's adaptive ways of minimizing stresses or anxieties. If properly recognized and understood, your child will be able to develop work-arounds.

 I need to reemphasize that it is very important for mothers to constantly re-affirm that their child isn't responsible for their serious literacy difficulties or for the interpersonal issues that arise from them. Mothers should also assure their child that all of the important people in their lives understand the nature and origin of their difficulties and can empathize with them!

In my experience, it is necessary to remind mothers that it is critical to let others know how to minimize their child's stresses. Especially in school, teaching the teacher how to maximize their child's capacity to access the curriculum and learn is vital.

Achieving this requires a lot of work for parents, family, friends and teachers. Seeking and developing appropriate accommodations is extremely important.

Most dyslexics will gradually and finally learn, and once they do, they are often better than children without dyslexia! However, many children will still learn slowly. Their writing and spelling can be almost as bad as their reading. But every dyslexic is unique and special and will advance at their own pace.

There are always layers of other emotions deep down inside and it can be serious – think depression, anxiety and addictions. This is not meant to frighten only to educate. Knowing is an important step in helping and understanding.

EMOTIONAL DEVELOPMENT

Research has shown that your child's emotional development can affect success or failure in learning.

I don't know that
I don't know

I know that I
don't know

I know that I
know

Knowing what we don't know
is one of the keys of success.

• •

Learning to be in control of present and future experiences, actions and the amount of effort put into overcoming difficulties is a necessary skill for your child, which is difficult to learn. Creating a plan dependent on the awareness of the right thing to do in specific situations is essential in overcoming issues.

Your success will depend largely upon a sense of identity created by both the family of the dyslexic and the dyslexic herself. A "team" effort is very important.

Recent research shows that there may be a link between Asperger's syndrome (high-functioning autism) and dyslexia. These autistic-type signs cannot be overlooked! Be on guard.

Many children with dyslexia (80% – 90%) have large amounts of social anxiety and other high-functioning problems. Mothers must be aware that social and emotional issues can be more of a problem than dyslexia itself.

Children with reading difficulties at nine years of age can have a significantly worse working memory at 18 years of age. Word fluency tasks, executive function and spelling problems can also suffer.

Knowing this in advance prepares both the child and the advocate to deal with these problems.

Adult dyslexics may still have difficulties – especially in situations such as written examinations and social interactions.

A common and powerful negative for your child is the denial of the thrill of success.

Feeling successful is the single greatest motivator towards learning and the most significant basis on which self-esteem is built.

When you feel like giving up,
look back at how far you've come.

Be strong. Stay on your path.
Never stop going.

I continually remind mothers that their children with dyslexia find themselves facing literacy challenges many times a day, every day for many, many years. This may occur outside the home and involve people of high emotional significance to the child, i.e. parents, peers, teachers, friends and schoolmates.

As your child grows older, she will become increasingly aware of how much value adults and peers place on these literacy skills. She will learn how much these skills may affect her future life and how disruptive they can be in terms of learning, home life, job success and marital happiness. It will become apparent that alcoholism, drug addiction and mental health challenges are common.

The only thing you can predict is the lack of predictability. What should be done? Proactively developing a Plan B and Plan C can often avoid feelings of anxiety and fear when the "normal" Plan A doesn't work.

By learning how to develop self-awareness and acceptance, mothers can analyze and learn how to support themselves. Never forget, things do get better!

I have noticed that many mothers find solace in prayer. Pick your favorite way to find comfort, emotional release and support.

Dyslexia can be regarded as more serious for some and mild for others. Often, different aspects of the many challenges will show up at different times. Understanding the underlying problem in short-term memory, speech and sound recognition needs to be emphasized.

Mommy, never forget I came this way. I really WANT to be like you! I HOPE you and I will be able to get through this. Remember, Pablo Picasso said, "He can who thinks he can..."

Thoughts on Emotional Regulation:

 Children with dyslexia may easily and rapidly shift from one emotion to the next. Others may have trouble regulating impulsive thoughts or actions. They must learn how to build self-awareness. **One of their best tools is having loving parents.**

Fortunately, some children learn to handle their emotional sensitivity and can avoid becoming overwhelmed, or engaged in negative social interactions. Nevertheless, your child may be so deeply affected that they become depressed or suffer from anxiety. It seems as if a child with dyslexia is constantly in motion.

 Lack of school, job or social success will to add to their emotional burden. Children with dyslexia who have been humiliated and shamed by family members, teachers and peers will feel rejected. They may then be motivated to take criticism to heart because of their humiliating experiences. Combining this with their ultrasensitive emotions and vulnerability may result in emotional abuse and can lead to long-term emotional problems and scarring. Children with dyslexia need to be understood.

DEPRESSION AND DESPONDENCY

I constantly remind mothers that depression is a common symptom for children with dyslexia, because these children tend to be very sensitive, very vulnerable and very hurt by rejection. Mothers are at high risk because of the intense feelings of sorrow and pain. That, plus a lack of self-esteem, can cause them to turn their anger outwards. Even worse, they may turn that same anger inward and become severely depressed.

Depression has four similar characteristics. Experiencing these can be compared to being emotionally lost in the swamp:
1. Negative personal thoughts
2. Do not appreciate their family
3. Do not enjoy life
4. View the future as bleak

The answer is to keep communication open and non-judgmental. This will make the child feel safe and loved and in turn both the adult and the child will feel better.

Depressed dyslexic adults often have different symptoms than adults that do not have dyslexia and are depressed.

Instead of feeling lethargic, or talking about how sad they feel, dyslexics may become more active or misbehave to cover up painful feelings. In the case of masked depression, they may not seem obviously unhappy.

Both children and adults who are depressed tend to have three (3) similar characteristics:
1. Tend to have negative thoughts about themselves, i.e., a negative self-image.

2. Tend to view the world negatively. They are less likely to enjoy the positive experiences in life. This makes it difficult to have fun.

3. Most depressed youngsters have great trouble imagining anything positive about their future.

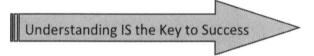

Understanding IS the Key to Success

Remember, the depressed dyslexic not only experiences great pain in their present circumstances, but also forsesees a life of continuing failure and pain. You are their lifesaver. They are like orchids which require a lot of gentle care and mothers are the gardeners they need.

Dyslexia affects all of life and family, and it is not something which can be outgrown. People don't grow out of dyslexia. If you are dyslexic, you will be so for life but there are reasons for **HOPE**.

Eventually things do improve and success and happiness will follow. However, the difficulties may become harder to manage in secondary school.

> After a usually difficult high school experience, life does get better. College is easier to deal with because motivation develops as a result of setting goals and objectives.

May the tide that is entering
Even now the Lip of our understanding,
Carry you out beyond the Face of fear.
May you kiss the wind Then turn from it
Certain that it will love you back.
May you open your eyes to water,
Water waving forever and
May you in your innocence
Sail through this to that.

—Lucille Clifton "blessing the boats"

MATERNAL ISSUES

· · · · · · · · · ·

*When you feel lost, remember
who you're doing it for.*

FRUSTRATION

What About My Feelings and Frustrations?	How Can I help Reduce My Worries and Help My Child?
You may find it baffling, frustrating, exasperating and even heartbreaking to watch your child struggle with reading.	Recognize that your feelings are natural.
	Learning more about your child's difficulties and that will help you to cope.

You may wonder if your child is just lazy or "deliberately obstructive."	Learn to recognize the signs of anxiety.
You may find it difficult not to correct or interfere.	Give your child more control by allowing him to choose his own books and letting him get ready for reading by himself.
You may find it difficult to avoid getting upset or angry and it may be difficult to hide such emotions from your child.	Help your child to relax by making reading a pleasant time. Talk about the story, introduce humor and make connections between the story and your child's experience.

Identify what words of compassion you would have wanted to hear as a child and what your child needs now!

This might include, for example, "I'm sorry for your pain," "You didn't deserve what happened to you," "You are only human, we all make mistakes," or "It's okay to feel what you feel."

Mothers should know that they need to be open to self-compassion and self-empathy. This means recognizing, being aware and accepting any hurts that originated from past wounds of their own – especially those that may contribute to their tendency toward guilt and shame.

Make peace with the earlier version of yourself. Acknowledge that it is easy to beat yourself up in hindsight over the limited awareness, which you may have had in the past.

Developing compassion as an antidote for shame will require awareness, acceptance, patience and overall, a commitment to resolve issues. It is difficult to decrease one's vulnerability to self-destructive anger.

Unfortunately, shame or guilt itself can undermine the practice of self-compassion and cause you to reject compassion from others. Addressing this challenge may require the assistance of a mental health professional.

Mothers need to help their children embrace self-compassion as an antidote to guilt and shame.

A background of guilt and shame undermines the energy needed for focused attention.

Overcoming guilt and shame can foster self-assertion and expression. This enhances the capacity to be more fully present with yourself and others. It reduces vulnerability to anger and ultimately, helps you to live a more fulfilling life.

ADVERSITY

Mothers may feel that being overwhelmed is a fact of life. The list of daily things that must be accomplished can feel like a millstone around your neck. This can lead moms to com-

• •

promises in many areas, including every day common issues. When this happens, the whole family is impacted and never really understands all of the mother's emotions and problems.

What mothers need the most is time, yet it is the one thing they don't have. As a physician, I have written many prescriptions for moms that say:

> Get more "me time" twice a day forever. And add a little more before a well-deserved sleep.

Self-Awareness is necessary in order to anticipate and modulate life's curveballs.

Following with Acceptance, Analysis...

...and develpment of an Action plan the 4 A's will help with success!

> Mothers of dyslexics never have real "me" time.

Mothers frequently have negative feelings such as denial, frustration, guilt and stress after learning that their dreams to have a "*perfect*" child will be unfulfilled.

This can also result in frustration and disappointment when children fail to meet their high expectations. Many mothers of children with dyslexia will experience depression and anxiety due to their worries about their child's future life consequences, academic performance and even marriage.

Mom, you are not alone! Be aware of and work to change the expectations, so that no one feels HOPELESS.

Mothers may frequently have to be concerned with inappropriate behavior. This behavior can affect the child's self-esteem and his ability to socialize with peers, friends and family. These issues will dramatically increase the mother's emotional intensity.

Examples are:
Fatigue/Lack of Sleep/Poor Sleep Quality
Changes in Daily Routine
Loss of Appetite
Weight Loss or Weight Gain

Much of a mother's concern begins with uncooperative or unconcerned teachers. Mothers may experience negative issues and emotions related to dealing with the special classes in an often-unexperienced educational system, as well as being extremely stressed by the need for the child's success at school.

You must have persistence and determination in order to achieve success. Lack of cooperation and concern among teachers causes maternal adversity. It is often due to the educators' lack of knowledge, **awareness** and **understanding.**

Teachers are frequently overloaded or unable to help. Maternal frustration and anger are justified! Being a strong advocate is most important but difficult to accomplish. Children with dyslexia, in my opinion, should not be mainstreamed. I am a firm believer in special needs classes.

It is very important to identify your child's emotional wounds from childhood and adolescence. These may lead to serious feelings of rejection, social anxiety, social phobia and depression.

This frequently results in great maternal frustration and fear.

Real Issues That May Happen:

- Having to choose between one child getting mental health care and another getting speech therapy.

- Being in debt due to outside professional assistance.

- Losing a retirement fund that was built up over 24 years, or a college fund that was begun over 17 years ago.

- Having to choose between a psychiatrist, psychologist or "whoever," solely based on cost.

- Having to choose between marital therapy for the parents or bankruptcy.

Tough choices!

Many guilt-ridden mothers internalize their feelings. They turn anger inward and blame themselves for their child's problems. This invariably leads to frustration and depression which can be very difficult to resolve, if ever.

> Clinically, I have often noted that depression comes with attendant feelings of inadequacy, helplessness and **HOPELESSNESS**, which may lead to maternal emotional withdrawal, alcoholism, drug dependency (often sleeping pills), personal injury and thoughts of suicide.

Parents, especially mothers, are often affected quite profoundly because a child has difficulties, some of which frequently vary from day to day.

Key Strategies for overcoming Maternal Guilt:

- ♥ Practicing meditation can be a powerful way to become less reactive to thoughts or feelings.

- ♥ Intentional mindfulness can strengthen and calm you.

● ●

♥ Expanding your compassionate self will involve the gradual development of a positive vocabulary that will reflect forgiveness and self-acceptance.

All parents will face many significant difficulties due to their child's dyslexia. These will result in very strong emotions! Everyone is affected and no one is immune. Marital difficulties are frequent.

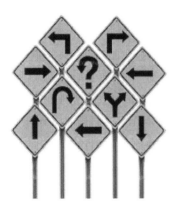

Initially, mothers and fathers may feel confusion about the nature of dyslexia and find it difficult to comprehend. This is totally understandable.

Parents feel great *concern* about what the future will hold for their child. They *worry* about whether their child will be successful in school, marriage or employment and whether they will be able to achieve their full potential.

> Parents may be frightened that if their child is unsuccessful at school, they may be drawn to other undesirable directions, e.g. crime, drugs, bad company, etc. This worry is very common.

Moms will frequently (almost always) feel anger toward the school system because they are unable to get teachers to understand and appreciate their child's problems.

Parents might also show anger towards other family members if they feel they are not helping the dyslexic child enough or do not appreciate and **understand** the problem fully. The

bulk of the work needed to support dyslexics almost always falls on the shoulders of the mother.

It needs to be emphasized that mothers will suffer frustration due to feelings of helplessness – largely because they are unable to get their voices heard at school. This maternal adversity can get worse if mothers feel that their child's teacher is incapable of helping their child at a satisfactory level.

Mothers will frequently exhibit overprotectiveness due to watching their child struggle daily with dyslexia. As hard as it is, children need to learn how to adapt to daily issues on their own. Be very careful here – overprotectiveness can easily become extreme.

Mothers will frequently feel exasperation and despair because of the difficulty of convincing "professionals" that it is necessary to **understand** dyslexia and how it affects their child.

However, what is often worse is when the appropriate help can't be obtained, or the mother doesn't feel as if their voice is heard.

Dyslexia can frequently lead to arguments between family members, teachers and friends. This produces great tension which can upset and ruin relationships.

Teachers and professionals need to be aware of these factors and act sympathetically when dealing with parents. Parents must try to make teachers aware of their presence and concern for their child. Weekly (Friday for example) connections through email are very helpful at keeping communications open and timely.

It is very important to realize that dyslexics have three speeds:

Slow, Slower but NEVER STOP.

SELF-BLAME
Another major obstacle to developing self-compassion is the tendency of parents to blame themselves for their child's condition. Self-blame is corrosive to a person's spirit.

Tormenting themselves about time taken away from the child because of a stressful job, discipline which was used when the child was young, or thinking about what could have been done wrong that caused the child's problems is pointless and helps no one.

You cannot change whatever happened in the past, but you can look forward. Forgive yourself, if you can, for your perceived sins.

Rationally, you may grasp that your child's condition is not your fault, but the guilty feelings and attempts to "make up for" what happened, persist. Or perhaps you think that if your own emotional pain matches whatever pain your child is going through, then somehow, you've made the situation better.

If guilt and self-judgment are preventing you from taking self-care steps that would benefit you and your child, finding a therapist who can support and help you develop a more positive self-image is important.

Remember, too, that modeling self-compassion is one of the most valuable gifts you can give your child. Dyslexics have a tendency to be hard on themselves and take blame for their parents' worry and unhappiness.

Only you can teach your child that every human being is lovable and worthy of kindness. You can teach your son or daughter that it is normal and expected to be kind to yourself, to forgive yourself, and to have realistic expectations of yourself.

> YOU ARE THE MOST BEAUTIFUL THING I KEEP INSIDE MY HEART
> —Unknown Author

A hug is the shortest distance between friends

*"Hugs can do great amounts of good,
especially for children."*
—Princess Diana

Survive and Thrive: A Lifelong Plan

It takes a village to raise a child, but it takes an army to raise atypical ones. After self-compassion, the most important thing to understand is that you can't do this alone. I'd like to share with you the following time-tested ways to assemble your support team for the years ahead.

Cultivate Your Extended Family

Just as you are not merely a daughter or son any longer, your mom and dad are no longer just parents. They have another role, as grandparents, so don't assume that they are the same people who raised you. Consider the possibility, too, that they might be eager for a reason to connect with you in a different way. Your child might be the bridge that allows them to express their love, regardless of your rocky past relationship.

Siblings are another potential source of support. What might have been rancorous sibling rivalry can evolve into something altogether different if your brother or sister wants to be an aunt or uncle to your child.

You may see a side of this person that you never noticed before. Or they may develop an empathy and generosity of spirit they didn't know they possessed. This is a recurring theme among the families with whom I work.

Become Part of a Community

Research backs this up: Children who grow up in a faith-based community and feel embraced and welcomed by that community, are emotionally better off. If religion is not for you, consider a cultural or secular group that has the same community-focused features. The goal of raising any child is to enable him or her to become integrated into the larger community.

Religious or cultural communities can help dyslexics gain confidence, mingle with other children and adults, and learn how to contribute their effort to the group. There are a lot of obvious benefits for parents, too. If you are not the joining type, try to develop new relationships that can nurture and support your family within a group setting. Even joining a local political grassroots organization that makes the world a better place can be inspirational on a personal and family level (Eichenstein).

KEY STRATEGIES FOR OVERCOMING MATERNAL SHAME

- ♥ Become attuned to the script of your inner dialogue and expand your capacity to observe, but not react to it. Self-awareness.

● ●

♥ Develop greater inner-compassion; be able to choose compassion as an alternative and cultivate a dialogue of increased self-acceptance of your humanity. This means recognizing that, like all humans, you have flaws and weaknesses, make mistakes and suffer. You are not alone, even when you feel that you are. Self-awareness, acceptance, analysis and action can be most helpful.

♥ Allow yourself to "witness" and mourn your wounds. This requires the ability to identify and sit with the pain associated with your hurts—both current and past. How about self-empathy and self-compassion? They work.

♥ Forgive your "former self" for feelings, thoughts or actions which you regret. In hindsight, it is easy to beat yourself up about the insight that you lacked at an earlier age.

Important Observations

Frustration with prolonged failure at school will result in feelings of insecurity and lack of confidence. These can have profound effects on social status, friendship patterns, acceptance and the ability to adjust in new settings. Aggressive and antisocial behavior may occur. Maternal alertness is essential.

Does it seem that a child with dyslexia is a puzzling muddle of strengths and weaknesses? They are! But their excellent intuition will become a strength which will help them in the future in many ways.

Variability may be their normal in some children. Knowledge of this fact will lead to better understanding.

Mothers who see and experience these varying emotions in their child often feel bewildered and unprepared which may lead to lack of confidence, low self-esteem, frustration and even depression. Mothers need a support person, someone with whom to share experiences and struggles. This must not be neglected!

Leaving this need unmet can result in fear, social nervousness, isolation, reluctance to take part in conversations and a tendency to avoid people. Some mothers are naturally susceptible to being a loner or an outsider; sometimes this may cause them to seem unfriendly or difficult. This can lead to a vicious and unrelenting cycle of pain for both moms and their children.

Having supportive friends at this stage of your life is critical: the nonjudgmental friend who brings over dinner when you're falling apart; the friend who's going to take your kids for a walk with your dog so you can go take a shower; the friend who will come over at the drop of a hat to have a cup of coffee with you when you're feeling lonely.

Isolation, being overwhelmed, needing a break and loneliness are all issues with which parents of dyslexic children really struggle. Building connections with other people who **understand** your situation and can help support you is very important.

To find a good friend you need to be a good friend. Remember to give to others and nourish your dear relationships. Consider joining an advocacy group or support group for families with dyslexics.

Be prepared to deal with frustration, depression, anxiety and other emotions.

Frequently remind yourself that these feelings will come sooner than later.

You will need a friend to reach out to. Find someone who has some experience.

Choose someone who understands what it means to have self-empathy and self-compassion.

MATERNAL NEEDS
Self-Awareness 💜 Self-Empathy
Self-Compassion

4-Step Process for Taking Charge:

1. Notice, name and normalize the arousal or anxious feelings, as opposed to the worried thoughts. Begin to see the feelings as useful.

2. Stop listening to the internal noise of worry by reminding yourself that you are in charge. Tell yourself that the emotion is not the truth and that just because you feel as though your survival is threatened, doesn't mean it is. When the brain registers that worry will not help the situation, it will kick in, take charge and begin to reason. Stop and think!

3. Allow time to reset. Use deep-breathing, relaxation or mindfulness exercises to move out of worry (fight/flight/freeze) mode. Time to breathe!

4. Get your brain back in charge. Step back into the discomfort, manage the uncertainty and problem solve.

My Recommendations:

- **Keep worried thoughts to yourself.** Manage your worries away from your child. Be the one who is warm and nurturing. Teach yourself self-regulation skills. Maximize interactions when you can. **Don't worry; worrying can be lethal.**

- **Keep expectations in line with what is.** Acknowledge the struggle when you see it. Recognize that the expectations and demands people and society make on your child may not be developmentally appropriate. Consider their individual differences and skill levels. It may take many tries to be able to self-regulate successfully. (Awareness)

- **Practice mindfulness.** Mindfulness is the simple but powerful act of slowing down. Remain in the present and pay attention to one thing at a time. Being mindful improves access to the brain and helps you feel better. It helps build self-management skills and increases confidence, performance, the quality of relationships and peace of mind for moms and their children.

- **Slow down, simplify and hang out.** Children with dyslexia need increased opportunities for unstructured, media-free time and free play. Provide age-appropriate supervision – not constant adult direction and micromanagement.

At the end of the day, remind yourself that you did the best you could today, and that is good enough.

- **Get enough sleep.** For optimal functioning, children and adolescents need between 9 and 11 hours of sleep per night.

ANGER STYLES

Over many decades I have observed several different anger styles. Some overlap with each other.

Stuffing – Do you "stuff" your anger?

- Do you tend to avoid direct confrontation?
- "Stuffers" can deny anger. They may not admit to themselves or to others that they are angry.
- "Stuffers" may not be aware that they have the right to be angry.

Some reasons mothers' "stuff":

- Fear of hurting or offending someone
- Fear of being disliked or rejected
- Fear of losing control of their emotions
- Feeling it's inappropriate (not okay) to be angry
- Feeling unable to cope with such a strong, intense emotion
- Fear of damaging or losing a relationship
- It's a learned behavior (but it can be unlearned!)
- Trying to use a different style of anger management than the one you were raised with

Escalating

Do you "escalate" to rage? Do you try to control, but lose control? "Escalators" blame people and can become the "provoker." Escalating often leads to abusive situations.

Some reasons you escalate are:

- Feeling you have no other choice
- To demonstrate an image of strength/power
- To avoid expressing underlying emotions
- Fear of getting close to someone

- It's a learned behavior (but can be unlearned!)
- Lack of communication skills

Consequences/Problems
1. Anger comes out—regardless
2. Impairs relationships
3. Compromises physical and mental health
4. Desired results may be short-term
5. Possible physically destructive behavior
6. Legal ramifications

> "While there are challenges to being dyslexic, there are also enormous strengths."
> —Lisa Maska

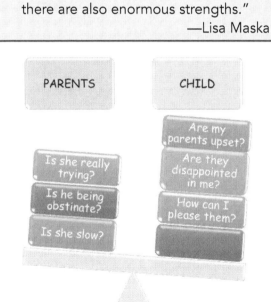

Mom, do you know how to "manage" your anger?

An important question every mother should ask herself is, "Am I allowing **anger** to mobilize me in positive directions?" Open, honest and direct expression is usually the most effective way for moms to manage anger with anyone. It's easier said than done. When expressing anger directly, mothers **must** keep these important skills in mind:

- Remind yourself that anger is a normal human emotion. It's okay to feel angry!
- What was the trigger event? Is this good timing for the listener?

- Remember your body language: firm voice, moderate tone, direct eye contact, maintain personal "space," establish an even eye-level with your child.

- Don't blame your child.

- Focus on the specific behavior that triggered your anger.

- Avoid "black or white" thinking.

- Use such phrases as "I feel angry when…" and "I feel angry that…" when expressing your anger.

- Don't drag in old issues now.

- Check for possible compromises.

- After open, honest and direct expression, close the discussion and then move on.

Many mothers tend to hold their feelings inside rather than talk about them. Dyslexic children are more likely to have an angry outburst as the pressure increases (much like a pressure cooker).

A mother's anger may be a defense to avoid painful feelings. It may be associated with failure, low self-esteem and feelings of isolation. Anger may be related to anxiety about situations over which mothers have no control. Angry defiance by moms may be associated with feelings of sadness, depression, frustration and anger.

Mothers need to be careful because anger and sadness are very close to one another. Maternal meltdowns do occur.

It is important to remember that mothers can experience an emotion as sadness, while their child expresses it as anger.

Parents need to distinguish between anger and aggression, although this can sometimes be difficult. Understand that anger may be okay sometimes. Look at the situation before deciding.

> Mom, do not become isolated.
> Stay connected.
> Have at least one good friend.

Maternal Personal Experience:

I have found in the early stages; many mothers may be in denial of the dyslexia because they perceived that their child was normal. Nevertheless, they may be able to accept the situation after conversations with medical professionals and family members, or praying to God.

One of my mother's showed me how she initially denied her child's condition:

"Teachers complained that my son was too slow...one day I saw that my son wrote words with p's and b's incorrectly... my husband said he looked like a dyslexic child...I said no... impossible. He is an intelligent boy...he has a good memory and is talkative...Then after my son was diagnosed, my husband and I had to accept it...I have to tolerate with what was given to me."

PERSEVERANCE

I have known mothers who frequently say that their husbands have limited time with their children. While most dyslexia problems will be managed by mom, dads can be helpful and become a strong partner who makes a difference.

This is illustrated by a mother I know:

"It's very hard because it is only me at home during the weekend. My husband is busy. By the time I want to teach my son, I need to wash dishes, clean up the kitchen, wash clothes and many other jobs...Sometimes when I want to teach my son his little sister comes in to disturb us...there are too many things to do at the same time. I feel helpless."

> Mom, you need a friend
> who is dealing with the same problems,
> who can understand and be
> a support person.

Many mothers complain that their daily life pattern is disturbed frequently, if not every day. I have never heard a mom with a dyslexic child say, "I have free time." The first thing that moms usually do after coming home from work or from picking up their child from school is sit together and talk about how the day went. This is a way for the child to regroup and destress by sharing any negative, confusing or fearful experience which may have happened.

Pre-planning will help your child recognize and encourage them to persist in their efforts. Determination should be encouraged. Very often, children need to be helped with motivation and understanding.

This whole book can be summarized in three words:

 UNDERSTANDING

 HOPE

 LOVE

Your child's body has very specific sensory needs, different from those of most people.

Not only do dyselxics require different types of input to balance their sensory systems, they need to recognize the sensory input and deal with it differently.

Personal Experience:

Most mothers know and **understand** that their dyslexic child's behavior is different compared to that of other children, especially when doing any academic-related tasks.

They are often described as:

1. giving up easily
2. getting frustrated
3. being bored

This requires parents to keep supporting and encouraging them. Maternal fatigue often sets in. For example, a mom described:

"I need to be more patient with his behavior...he likes to argue when I talk to him. He will throw books...I always need to praise and give verbal support to him; only then will he do his homework."

Everybody is a genius, but if you judge a fish by
its ability to climb a tree, it will live its whole
life believing that it is stupid.
—Albert Einstein

SUPPORT NETWORK

Mom, here's what you must know about stepping stones and your journey. While there are momentous highs and lows, the flat-out truth is a moms' life is very hard in almost every way possible. When children are young, mothers will have to work hard to:

- Identify and recognize their child's possible issues

- Understand what the identification means

- Understand that the school is using a research-based OSFA (one size fits all) remediation program

- Encourage, if possible, extra after-hours tutoring with someone who really knows what they're doing

- Provide proper homework support

- Understand that children should be kids and live as normal and happy of a life as possible, given their struggles.

- Be a very strong advocate.

DIFFICULTIES

. . . .

Strong people
rarely have an easy past.

What makes you vulnerable
makes you beautiful.
—Brene' Brown

ADJUSTING
Mom, why do I have problems with people?

Change can be challenging for everyone. Your child may have a hard time moving from one activity to another. They prefer things to stay the same. Sameness is something a dyslexic child likes, as well as consistence, and predictability. New things should be introduced slowly; preferably one at a time.

 Your child can be inflexible when it comes to considering other people's points of view or different ways of doing things. This need to keep things the same will often end up isolating them. Their inflexibility can be emotionally challenging and increase the feelings of loneliness and rejection. It can become a vicious cycle.

Change brings difficulty. Your child is less prepared for the unexpected. This brings new learning hurdles, job demands and social challenges. Without being aware, a child will blame the other person for their lack of flexibility. Understand the basis for this difficulty with adjusting to change. Dyslexic children need and prefer sameness.

The unique challenges of your child are not something to work "out" of them, but to work through and embrace. Remember, they came this way! (and there's a good chance you did, too!)

Your child's body has very specific sensory needs, different from those of most people. Not only do they require different types of input to balance their sensory systems, but they need to recognize their sensory input and deal with them differently.

Realism, awareness, acceptance and understanding are keys to successfully build self-confidence.

LOSS OF CONFIDENCE

Mom, how will dyslexia affect my self-confidence in school and elsewhere?

A child with dyslexia may say, "I am insecure and full of fear. I need your help!"

Most people with dyslexia in their family know how much of a struggle reading and writing can be, but dyslexia can also severely affect social skills and throw long-term scarring into the mix.

The following page contains a list of some common social skill challenges which can help to aid in the development of these important skills:

*Dyslexics don't understand jokes or sarcasm. Telling jokes or funny stories at the dinner table can give an opportunity to practice responding properly. Teach your child simple things like smiling and seeming interested in the story. Eye contact helps tremendously!

*Dyslexics have trouble finding the right words. Especially if they feel strongly about a subject or need to respond quickly. They need time to think before responding and slow down the overall pace of the conversation.

*Dyslexics may miss social cues. An important one is body language. A great role-playing exercise for this is to watch their favorite shows with the volume turned off. Try to guess how a character is feeling based on their body language and facial expressions. Occasionally using subtitles with the sound on can also be a way to connect body language with dialogue.

*Dyslexics often hesitate messaging friends. They may shy away from texting because of the difficulty understanding abbreviations. Some are based on spelling ("I don't know" = idk) and others on how letters and numbers sound ("later" = l8tr).

*Dyslexics need to remember things accurately in order to increase self-confidence. They usually have trouble with short-term memory. Helping improve memory skills by playing games is a fun way to work on these. Keep sticky pads handy or use an app on a smartphone. These can be used to instantly record something which needs to be remembered.

Dyslexia has been referred to as a "gift." However, very few moms experience it as such.

Dyslexia is a lifelong challenge that can improve, but it is not a gift for most! A good gift is social involvement with peers: think Girl Scouts, Boy Scouts, choir, clubs, etc. This is very important!

> The main factor that determines whether someone will thrive or not is the presence of a supportive and encouraging person in their life—like a loving mom.

HYPERSENSITIVITIES
Mom, why do I *feel* so much?

I have noticed that dyslexic children are often overwhelmed by too much environmental stimuli (e.g., background noise, bright lights, more than one person talking at a time, crowds, visual overload, side conversations, reading and listening at the same time).

Many such children also have specific sensitivities to their environment, such as certain fabrics they cannot wear, foods they cannot tolerate, smells they cannot bear and not wanting to be touched. These issues are called Sensory Processing Disorders. Hypersensitivity, vulnerability and auditory issues may be very common and need evaluation. Mothers should do their best to be aware of these issues.

Many children with dyslexia see themselves as much more emotionally sensitive than other people. This sensitivity in its most extreme form, can be difficult to tolerate and even overwhelming. High levels of emotional sensitivity **may be a blessing** and a curse.

The positive features of this trait can lead to greater **understanding**, which in turn can help build meaningful relationships with others.

Your child may often be very intuitive, empathetic and in tune with both their own and other people's emotions. These strengths can also be a weakness due to the propensity to be overwhelmed. A child with dyslexia will almost never forget a bad experience! Learning to let go of a negative situation and move on with life will be a great help in the future.

> Failure to deal with these issues will lead to permanent emotional scarring.

I would like to remind you that your child's feelings can cross the line into aggression, which can cause social rejection and/or emotional overload. They may be unaware that their behavior has turned aggressive and believe that they are only trying to make their point of view known and **understood**.

SENSORY SENSITIVITIES
Mom, why am I so sensitive?

The opposite side of sensory-seeking is sensory sensitivities. Children with dyslexia, autism and Asperger's have difficulty filtering or modulating sensory input. This makes certain types of sensory information intolerable. The exact same sensory input might have no effect on a typical person, because their sensory system filters or modulates the input down to a tolerable level.

REMEMBER
Sensory overload has both emotional and physical consequences. Too much sensory input can cause anxiety, fear, panic and a feeling of helplessness, often leading to a shutdown or meltdown. Physical overload can cause everything from queasiness to unbearable pain.

My personal experience is that there are ways for mothers to reduce the impact of environmental sensory triggers. At home or in school, moms can frequently modify surroundings to remove or reduce triggers. This is essential. This may be necessary every day before going to school.

Most children with dyslexia have sensory sensitivities, such as visual, auditory, smell, taste and sound, but the type and intensity will vary greatly from one child to another.

It's common to have one or two senses that are especially sensitive while others are moderately sensitive. Noise is often the most frequent problem.

Light Sensitivities

The most common form of light sensitivity is from fluorescent lights. Not only do fluorescent lights emit a low-pitched hum, but they also tend to flicker in intensity. The light they give off can be harsh and overly intense.

Often, dyslexics will find it hard to concentrate in a room with fluorescent lighting. Unfortunately, most classrooms, offices, workplaces and stores have fluorescent lighting, making it hard to avoid.

Ideally, changing the light source to a cooler, less intense type or taking advantage of natural light sources is the best way to reduce the effects of light sensitivities. When this isn't possible, tinted sunglasses indoors is helpful.

> **TIP: A few adaptations:** wearing sunglasses outdoors (especially for driving), choosing living and work spaces with as much natural light as possible to eliminate the need for artificial light sources during the day, and watching television with a soft light on in the room to reduce the harshness of the screen.

> **REMEMBER**
> *Light sensitivities can be very serious.* Visual overload, especially from bright or flickering light sources, can cause nausea, headache, pain in the eyes, dizziness, disorientation, seizures and even anger or meltdowns.

SENSITIVITY TO SOUND

Not only does hearing seem to be overly sensitive, but there may also be difficulty turning it off. What most people's brains filter out as useless background noise, dyslexic brains register in a constant stream of incoming auditory data that is impossible to ignore.

It's not like they want to hear the person sitting next to them in the library chewing gum, typing or even just breathing, but they can't not hear it.

This barrage of sound often results in sensory overload in public places, especially crowded stores, restaurants and public transit. It can also make it difficult to follow conversations or make out speech in environments with a lot of background noise. This happens to me because of hearing loss – different, yet similar.

> "Eyes may be the windows to the soul,
> but windows are also helpful to the dyslexic."
> —Unknown Author

Your child may constantly have to ask strangers to repeat themselves. After learning about auditory processing difficulties, they may realize that using lip reading to augment hearing when it comes to **understanding** spoken language is very helpful.

If they can't see a person's mouth, they are more likely to have to ask them to repeat something.

• •

I have noticed that many dyslexics find that using noise-cancelling headphones or earbuds playing music **helps to reduce the risk of sound overload in public.**

This strategy can also help minimize an overdeveloped startle reflex, which is common in people with noise sensitivities. They may startle at the slightest provocation.

Loud sounds, on the other hand, not only provoke a startle reflex, but they can also be painful and bring on many of the same physical symptoms as light sensitivities.

SENSITIVITY TO SMELL AND TASTE

Smell and taste are controlled by chemical receptors on the tongue (taste) and in the nose (smell and taste). Often, some who have sensitivities in one area also have sensitivities in the other.

When it comes to food, the senses of taste and smell are closely linked. It's hard to imagine eating foods that smell repulsive. Often, just the smell of a particular food being prepared will trigger a gag reflex in someone with taste and smell sensitivities.

Many dyslexics eat a restricted diet because they find so many foods intolerable. For some, strong flavors or smells are triggers, while for others specific categories such as citrus, tomato or mint trigger sensitivities.

These types of sensitivities are very hard to overcome because the physical response to triggering tastes and smells can be over-powering. This makes it physically impossible to be near the food, let alone eat it. Fortunately, it's possible to create nutritious meals while sticking to a bland or restricted diet, if necessary.

All of this sounds simple, but it is NOT easy!
Just ask your child.

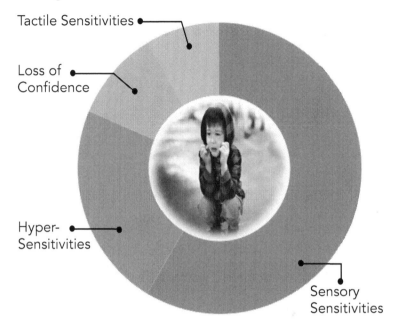

Tactile Sensitivities

Loss of
Confidence

Hyper-
Sensitivities

Sensory
Sensitivities

Beyond food sensitivities, smell sensitivities can extend to nearly anything in their daily environment. Some people have very specific smell triggers like wet animal fur, cigarettes, fish smell, deodorant, etc. Others are sensitive to strong smells, such as perfume, personal grooming products, detergents or air fresheners.

Many categories of smell sensitivities can be hard to avoid in public places because they are both common and hard to anticipate.

Carrying a familiar object with a pleasing smell, such as a handkerchief scented with vanilla or lavender, or pocket mints can be good emergency defenses against unexpected triggering scents.

Ultimately, these triggers do not go away!

TACTILE SENSITIVITIES

Tactile sensitivities, often called tactile defensiveness, are characterized by a negative reaction to a tactile stimulus that is generally considered non-irritating by most people. These include:

- Seams (especially in socks)
- Ruffles
- Synthetics
- Lace
- Tight/High Waist
- Wool
- Exposed elastics
- Tags
- Stitching felt against skin
- Collars that are too high, collars that are too open
- Sleeves that are anything other than standard (short- or long-sleeve length)

Many tactile sensitivities have also led to dozens of little quirks, most of which start in childhood. Some dyslexics don't like the feeling of water spraying on the face. Eating something messy with their fingers requires cleaning on a napkin between every bite. When skin gets too cold, it itches worse than a case of poison ivy.

If someone kisses them on the cheek, they frequently wipe the little wet spot from their face.

Dyslexics and people with mild autism (Asperger's) are often hypersensitive to light touch, but crave and seek out deep pressure touch.

Occupational therapists may recommend sensory tools like weighted blankets and lap pads to help people with tactile sensitivities to get the pressure they crave. Tight hugs and wedging our bodies into tight spaces are other ways of getting pressure. Heavy blankets frequently don't work. Borrow one before buying.

Some mild autistic people (Asperger's) share many traits in common with dyslexics. It truly is a spectrum. While they can have broadly similar experiences, the details of those experiences can be as different as night and day.

Yes, most have sensory sensitivities, but no one experiences the exact combination of sensitivities. Yes, everyone stims, but everyone's set of stims is unique. "Stim" means stimulation or a child's need for movement that is soothing. A few examples of stemming are:

- tapping your feet
- continually washing your hands
- washing with cold water
- rocking
- biting fingernails
- scratching your head
- doodling with a pen

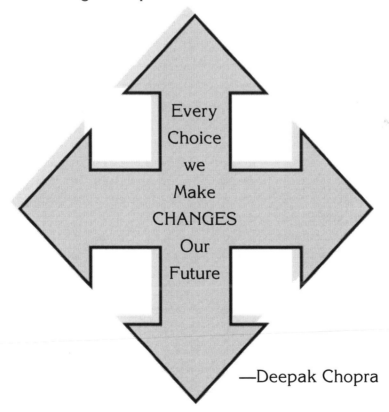

Every Choice we Make CHANGES Our Future

—Deepak Chopra

PESSIMISM
Mom, please help me with pessimism.

The treatment for pessimism and helplessness is often seen to be similar to the treatment for depression. If parents and teachers use optimism to change the negative thoughts (how they perceive and explain events to themselves) to more positive ones and remind the child that the negative thoughts are not realistic or true (e.g. you are special, it doesn't really matter if you didn't do well in that test), can help the child stay positive and more optimistic.

> If the lessons are more realistic and specific, and challenge the child's perceptions (e.g., challenging 'I am dumb') they can help their child form realistic thoughts, and the **effect will be worthwhile and long term**.

In school and other learning situations, students who are optimistic recover quickly from defeat. They learn to see defeat as a challenge to overcome and a temporary setback – specific to that experience and not pervasive.

However, those who are pessimistic will be depressed in defeat. They will see the defeat (failure) as permanent and pervasive. They can become depressed and stay that way for a long time. **They tend to see any setback as defeat**, and one defeat is like losing a war. Because they do not easily challenge defeat, they tend to shy away from trying such tasks again. Any new failure in similar tasks will confirm the helplessness and the negative thought pattern.

* HOPE!!! *
Advocate.
No matter how steep the climb.

Studies of Optimism versus Pessimism have shown that children with dyslexia who succeed in life and school are not always those who are the most talented, but those with the most optimistic frame of mind and supportive parents.

Treatments to turn pessimistic thoughts to optimistic ones start with investigating how your child perceives negative events. Try to recognize the emotional connection that results (e.g. failing in a task makes them feel sad and useless). They need **understanding**.

Start by investigating other meanings to events. Try to find realistic and possible ways forward to energize individuals.

The aim is to change important attributions...

FROM:

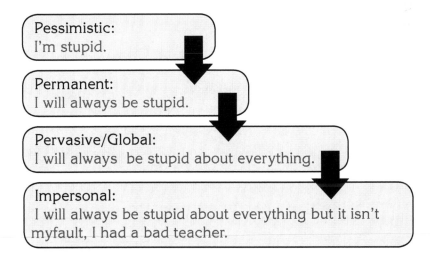

Pessimistic:
I'm stupid.

Permanent:
I will always be stupid.

Pervasive/Global:
I will always be stupid about everything.

Impersonal:
I will always be stupid about everything but it isn't myfault, I had a bad teacher.

TO:

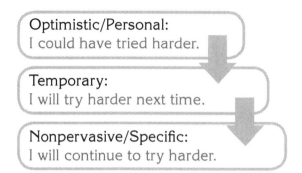

Optimistic/Personal:
I could have tried harder.

Temporary:
I will try harder next time.

Nonpervasive/Specific:
I will continue to try harder.

Allowing a chance to improve and try again, along with seeing themselves as the key to changing the situation is the best way to learn. Blaming others (e.g. I had bad teachers at school) rather than seeing themselves in an honest light (e.g. I need to spend personal time learning some new skills), will not allow the situation to improve.

The key is to change a negative view of events by being specific rather than global in feedback, e.g. *changing*, "I am useless at school" (global) to "I have problems in math, specifically algebra" (specific).

FEAR
Mom, why do I get so afraid?
Your child's early years are spent developing their self-image. These years can be full of frustrations. This can lead to your child's feelings of inferiority. If not dealt with quickly and helped, these emotions can grow to become ones of powerlessness and incompetence, which lead to fear! Then there is real trouble.

It has been suggested that children with dyslexia have feelings of inferiority that are developed by the age of 10. After this age, it becomes extremely difficult to help them develop a positive self-image. *This is a powerful argument for early intervention and homeschooling.*

Without regular success, children with dyslexia can develop a *very low tolerance* to difficult tasks, causing them to give up quickly when a project is perceived as being too hard. Frustration → depression → anger → bad stuff. Rejection is dangerous!!

■ **Fear of being found out.** The fear of being found out is particularly troublesome for many who were not diagnosed early or who received inappropriate support. Coping strategies were developed to hide the disability. They may develop gregarious personalities, or focus on other abilities that do not present learning barriers.

■ **Fear of judgment or criticism.** Your child may frequently fear the ridicule of others. Their fears often develop after being ridiculed by teachers, classmates or even family members. The most crushing of these criticisms usually relate to a perceived lack of intelligence or judgments about their degree of motivation and/or ability to succeed.

■ **Fear of rejection.** Children with dyslexia may frequently fear rejection if they are not seen to be as capable as others. If they come from a family where academic achievement is a basic expectation, fear of rejection is a very real concern. There may be a fear that their social skill deficits will preclude them from building meaningful relationships with others. This may lead to social rejection.

ISOLATION
Mommy, why don't I have any friends? Why don't you have friends?

☀ In my opinion, isolation is one of the worst consequences of having dyslexia or being a parent of a child with dyslexia. This is the principle cause of both adaptive and maladaptive coping strategies. Those who escape isolation and who are well-integrated socially have fewer problems, but some children with dyslexia and their mothers can spend their entire lives isolated from others. Isolation is dangerous and can be followed by discouragement, depression, anxiety and then anger. This can lead to self-destructive behavior.

✺ **Output communication can be faulty.** Dyslexics with language processing difficulties cause speech to create a "logjam" inside. Nonverbal behavior is very important and is often the part of speech that contains disturbing transmission errors. In the most severe cases of dyslexia, outward communication is almost nullified. Your child may present herself totally wrong, as completely unresponsive or even autistic.

✺ **Inward communication is faulty**. Your child with dyslexia may find it hard to process incoming speech from other people. Information processing delays and cognitive problems can mean it takes longer to receive and **understand** what others say. Yes, brain function can be slowed down, but your child can become adept if they are aware of the challenge and accept themselves without negative or defeated thoughts.

✺ In addition, dyslexics find it hard to read nonverbal behavior and can make the wrong interpretations of how other people behave. Unfortunately, they also tend to act on it. If mothers are aware of how their child is made up, they will be able to help. This is called **maternal understanding**.

✺ **Reading problems separate your child from the class.** They are withdrawn for remedial work, so they can fail to integrate properly. More isolation. This can make children with dyslexia anxious and depressed. Depression is a sufficient cause for rejection by others. Indeed, feeling different from others at a very early age is often reported. Difficulty with relationships can lead to loneliness.

ANXIETY

Anxiety may be your child's most frequent emotional symptom. This can be frustrating for mothers. Your child can become afraid because of constant frustration and confusion. These feelings can be made worse by any inconsistency in their life. They prefer predictability and sameness, which helps to pre-empt anxiety and/or depression.

Mothers can learn to anticipate failure! This requires awareness and acceptance. It is important to know that entering new situations causes extreme anxiety for your child.

Most emotional problems can be traced back to dyslexia. They seem to originate out of frustration with school or social situations. Social scientists have frequently observed that frustration produces anger.

It is also common to vent anger on parents. Mothers are particularly likely to feel the wrath. Often, children will sit on their anger during the school day to the point of being extremely passive, or overly critical.

Once the child is in a safe environment like home, the very powerful negative feelings erupt and are often directed toward parents or siblings.

A child with dyslexia will frequently anticipate failure when entering new situations. Know that anxiety can lead to very serious problems in life! Remember, being introduced to a new person can be very unnerving. Prepare beforehand to reduce the expected anxiety.

> **In the words of a Child with Dyslexia**
> *"I have spent years worrying about my inability to perform tasks and feeling acute anxiety about being found out, exposed and humiliated."*

Anxieties are a sign of the inability to 'narrow' thinking skills. This makes those with dyslexia very self-conscious, because it forces the brain to think only of one thing at a time, which can be disastrous for reading. Reading is a skill that requires a lot of things to happen at the same time.

Forgetting things from one moment to the next occurs because attention or focus is misplaced due to anxieties about failure. It slows or stops normal memory rehearsal and affects short-term memory. Think ADD.

> You have probably seen that your child's worries about failure may also motivate them to minimize or avoid these worries.

I have observed that a child with dyslexia may become reluctant to start a new school project and claim that they have lost books, or suddenly become chatty about anything and everything. Or perhaps they will offer to do some house-work or claim to feel "sick" ...anything to avoid doing the thing which needs to be done.

All of these issues may be signs of high levels of discomfort and can easily be misinterpreted as laziness. Your child may also start to guess wildly during difficult moments. This would be because any guess is better than none. At least this gives some chance of success.

Tips for Anxiety :

■ **Change the goal from trying to eliminate the worry to learning how to manage it.** You can never eliminate uncertainty and discomfort. So, help your child adjust their goal to learning how to manage his feelings in the face of uncertainty and discomfort.

■ **Keep the focus on managing and regulating the worry.** Your child won't focus during a meltdown; no one can. Your goal is to calm her down and get her brain back in control. Develop fun ways to discuss worry. Have matter-of-fact conversations about how to manage worry. Don't ever allow the worry to remain untreated.

■ **Listen to your child's alerts with interest, not alarm.** Be able to hear the despair and frustration without over focusing on the content. This is particularly challenging especially if he is expressing such things as, wanting to die. Such statements are important to take seriously, but curiosity without alarm allows for more accurate assessment. It will also allow children with dyslexia to experience their mother as more available and supportive.

PANIC ATTACKS
Mommy, I am having a meltdown! Help!!

I feel there is clear evidence that anxiety disorders are common in those with learning disabilities, specifically a child with dyslexia. Anxiety is serious and can lead to panic attacks. It is not often appreciated that anxiety can occur in response to subliminal stresses. This is serious anger that may ultimately trigger panic attacks or self-destructive behavior.

Panic attacks can seem to arise for no obvious reason. Traumatized dyslexics may endure a form of free-floating anxiety that comes **out of nowhere** in any situation involving change or literacy. This is most of the modern world. It is ever-present.

REMEMBER!
Panic attacks can affect children with
dyslexia in a stunning way!

They include irritability, restlessness, poor concentration and incoherence	to the degree

of being unable to say a word,	fear of going mad,	or being rooted to the spot.

My experience is that these children do not realize that there is a problem until some new and traumatic incident enters their lives. This can happen quickly.

Your child with dyslexia can have intense anger and frustration toward a teacher or parent, or may experience the emotional shock of being bullied by his peers because of dyslexia and all of its accompanying "oddities". It happens very fast – before they can realize something quite unidentifiable is terribly wrong.

Feelings can be devastating and comparable to the cold horror of receiving news that someone they liked has died; or the confirmation of a fatal illness. These experiences are seared into their brain. The memory retains its potency well into the future and creates a feeling of unending **HOPEless-ness**. Crying often helps. Reaching out helps.

Becoming self-aware, acceptance and **understanding** are keys to resolving or reducing this issue.

Mothers should be prepared for this to happen frequently. The explicit suddenness of these events and the accompany-

• •

ing feelings mean that in **one moment** the child can feel safe and predictable, and in the next dangerous and random.

Children with dyslexia can feel just as traumatized as if they were crushed in a car accident or hit by an unseen assailant. Lives can be marked by all the classic symptoms of post-traumatic stress disorder.

Dyslexics are very, very hypersensitive and especially vulnerable to rejection that can result in PTSD. They can't handle rejection. The PTSD leads to anxiety and inappropriate social behavior. Loss of boundaries can lead to a life that is compromised in many ways.

"It is as if all the colors and passions of a great and vivid painting are trapped behind a plain white paper."
—Neil Alexander-Passe

ANGER
"Mom, will it be easier to deal with anger if I don't think all anger is bad?"
Our goal should not be to repress or destroy angry feelings, but rather to accept the feelings and to help channel and direct them to constructive ends.

I strongly support the position that parents and teachers must allow children to feel all their feelings. It is critically important that adults' model for children acceptable ways of expressing their feelings. Strong feelings should not be denied and angry outbursts should not always be viewed as signs of serious problems. They should be recognized and treated with respect.

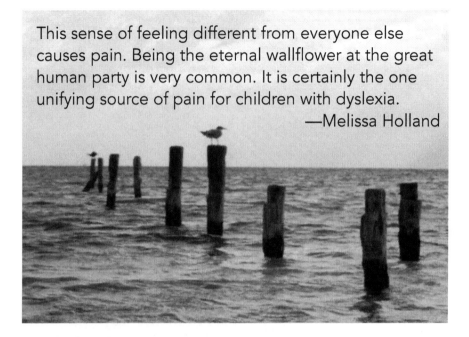

This sense of feeling different from everyone else causes pain. Being the eternal wallflower at the great human party is very common. It is certainly the one unifying source of pain for children with dyslexia.

—Melissa Holland

Sometimes the hardest part for mothers when handling anger issues is staying calm themselves. Remaining calm and learning ways to help recognize and manage your child's anger will give everyone more control over situations.

Helping children understand and manage their anger doesn't just make a difference in boost their self-esteem and help them find more success at school and with friends.

Strategies to try before, during and after a panic outburst:

♥ Define the triggers. Does your child have a shorter fuse at a certain time of day or after a certain activity? Observe their behavior and take notice. Knowing what upsets your child can help anticipate problems. Learn to talk about them in advance. Perhaps they are hungry or tired. Helping to recognize these basic needs is an important first step for you and your child. This is **understanding**, awareness and acceptance in action. Anticipate the triggers! Be prepared.

♥ Explain what you see. In the heat of the moment, children with dyslexia may not even be aware of how they're coming across to others.

♥ Help them identify their emotions by calmly saying things like, "You look really angry" or "You're raising your voice at me." "Let's talk later." Your child needs to learn how to be self-aware. This is the first step in learning self-control.

♥ Show empathy to build empathy. Showing your child **understanding** can help them get better at considering a different point of view. You can say something like, "You're not a morning person, and you can be a grouch when you wake up. I can see you're feeling frustrated. Let's talk about this after you've had some breakfast." **Most dyslexics need more sleep than non-dyslexics.**

♥ Don't engage. When your child is acting out in anger, try not to show any excessive interest. If they are safe say, "This situation is getting out of control. Let's calm things down by going into separate rooms. We can get back together again in a few minutes." This can stop their anger (and yours) from escalating. It also gives your child a way to save face and start again without the anger.

♥ Talk about angry episodes later. Some children with dyslexia can have a hard time being reflective in the moment. It can help to give your child some time to think about what happened before they talk about it. Refocusing is very helpful.

The kids who need the most love will ask for it in the most unloving of ways.
—Russell Barkley

Tips on Dealing with Anger:
- Praise your child when you catch them being good. Children need praise every day. They need to know they are appreciated. How you respond to appropriate behavior is just as important as how you respond to inappropriate behavior.

- Provide physical outlets and alternatives. Children need to be physical. Make sure they have appropriate places and times to do so.

- Remove your child from the situation, but do not isolate them. They may need to be alone or they may not. Redirect them toward appropriate behavior.

- Explain the situation. Tell them you accept their feelings, but explain why the behavior is not acceptable and provide alternatives.

- If you use a reward system, make sure the rewards are appropriate. Highlight the intrinsic value of the desired behavior. Rewards should not become an end, in and of themselves.

- Say "No!" Set limits.

> **In summary, it comes down to the 4 A's:**
> **Awareness, Acceptance, Analysis and Action Plan**

I think it should be emphasized that parents, teachers, counsellors and administrators need to remind themselves that they may not have been taught how to deal with a dyslexic's anger as a fact of life. They were led to believe that to be angry was to be bad. Mothers are often made to feel guilty for expressing anger. Stay cool, you will catch more flies with honey than vinegar.

> Mothers MUST BE CAREFUL to distinguish between behavior that indicates emotional problems and behavior that is normal.
> In dealing with angry children, moms' actions should be motivated by the need to protect and teach, not by a desire to punish

Parents and teachers should show your child that their feelings are accepted, while suggesting other ways to express themselves. An adult might say, "Let me tell you what some children would do in a situation like this..." It is not enough to tell your child what behaviors we find unacceptable; they must be shown an example of what they could have done instead.

Teachers and parents can positively reinforce a child's good behavior with statements like, "I know it was difficult for you to wait your turn" and "I am pleased that you could do it."

> I strongly suggest that mothers "catch" their child being good.
> Tell your child what behaviors please you.
> Respond to positive efforts and reinforce good behavior.
> Be observant and sensitive.

• •

Understanding parents can try to plan their child's surroundings so that certain things are less apt to happen. Stop a problem activity and substitute, temporarily, a more desirable one. If a child hates sports – don't make them do sports! Sometimes rules and regulations, as well as physical space, may be too confining.

Use closeness and touching. Move physically closer to them to curb their angry impulses. *Young children are often calmed by having an adult nearby.*

> Provide physical outlets and other alternatives that are helpful. It is important for your child to have opportunities for physical exercise and movement, both at home and at school.
>
> Manipulate their surroundings in a positive way.

Sometimes, all that your child needs is for you to help them regain loving control of their anger. Give them a **big hug** or show them another means of affection. Those with serious emotional problems may have trouble accepting affection.

It is my trust in you that allows me to vent anger. I know this can be very frustrating and confusing for you. I see you desperatley trying to help me. I feel your frustration and I want to help you, but I don't know what to do.

—Author Unknown

"While there are challenges to being dyslexic, there are also enormous strengths."

—Lisa Maska

GRIEF, BLAME, SHAME AND EMBARRASSMENT
Shame vs. Guilt

In my life I have learned that grief is an emotional force that cannot be controlled or predicted. It comes and goes on its own terms. Grief does not obey your plans or your wishes. It will do what it wants to you whenever it wants.

Grief has a lot to do with love and can change the very fabric of your life, even love. For a dyslexic mom, it can come any time. It is not something you can control. All you can do is accept the grief, **understand** it and be aware of the consequences. To resist, is to prolong the grief. It has been said that it's the price you pay for the love you have for your dyslexic child.

Mommy, why do I often feel embarrassed?

For some moms, it can be a great relief to know your child's diagnosis, while for other moms the label only serves to stigmatize them.

An accurate diagnosis of the difficulties is often unavailable for many and they feel a sense of shame, because of social anxiety, frustration and an absence of **understanding** of others!

In my life experiences, almost all children with dyslexia suffer from some guilt because they are "different." Guilt is one of the most powerful negative emotions. When experienced on a regular basis guilt can quickly turn to shame.

The very idea of shame is so embarrassing that most people do not even want to talk about it. Many moms argue that having a dyslexic child can lead to much guilt and worry for the mother. She may feel that it was her fault that her child was born "that way".

Shame has been observed not only in those who struggle to read, but also to spell and write. In addition to shame, children frequently experience humiliation and embarrassment when they are young. All of these negative emotions affect self-esteem.

The worst problem a child with dyslexia must face is not just reading, writing or even spelling, but a lack of **understanding shame and guilt**. Dyslexic students are commonly **humiliated** by teachers and made to do activities that put them in a bad light in front of their peers. For example, being asked to read aloud to the rest of the class or being sent out to receive special lessons. This results in peer-teasing and persecution. It can lead to feelings of shame, which can then lead to outbursts of anger.

> *The shame related to dyslexia is often a slow-drip trauma. Dyslexic children are made to feel "not normal" every day.*

The self-esteem of a dyslexic child in mainstream schools can be much lower than those children which are in schools for dyslexia, or home school. This suggests that mainstream settings allow for greater negative comparisons of worthiness. This can affect both motivation and self-concept. But with **understanding**, there is **HOPE**.

How to Process:

💚 Understand that the feelings of embarrassment deepen into shame and guilt.

💚 Be aware that embarrassment is often situational. Shame and guilt seem to seep throughout the whole personality and color the whole life.

💚 Realize that negative feelings can often cause children to hide difficulties.

💚 Be attentive. Rather than risking the label of "stupid" or being accused of laziness, children may deny their difficulties. They may become "the invisible student." Many children with dyslexia are very good at being invisible.

💚 **Children may be ashamed of the difficulties they are struggling to cope with.**

**The feeling of having a secret
is something that is very commonly
reported by dyslexics.**

Research indicates that dyslexia is caused by connection issues in the brain, not emotional or family problems. Many dyslexic preschoolers are happy and well adjusted.

Emotional problems tend to begin developing when early reading instruction does not match learning style. Over the years, frustration mounts as classmates surpass your child in reading skills. Mothers should be aware of this change, accept it and make plans to help.

The pain of failing to meet other people's expectations is surpassed only by the inability to achieve goals. This is particularly true of those children who develop perfectionistic expectations to deal with anxiety.

Children may grow up believing that it is terrible to make a mistake. This may further increase isolation and leads to down days, discouragement and depression.

Self-esteem is created by
experiences and begins to be
shaped from the earliest years of life.

DEALING WITH GUILT

Guilt is not a very good motivator. Overall guilt is in the category of negative feeling states – one of the "sad" emotions. These also include frustration, agony, greed and loneliness.

Guilt is an emotion that is experienced when someone is convinced that they have caused harm. This guilt comes directly from the thought that we are responsible for someone else's misfortune, whether or not this is the case.

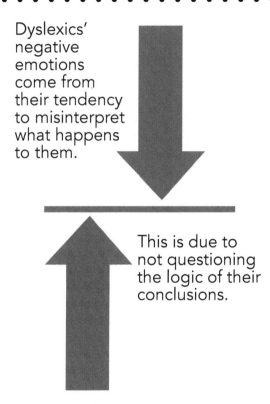

Dyslexics' negative emotions come from their tendency to misinterpret what happens to them.

This is due to not questioning the logic of their conclusions.

Dyslexics' negative emotions come from their tendency to misinterpret what happens to them. This is due to not questioning the logic of their conclusions.

Your child with dyslexia may be constantly plagued by guilt can be taught to recognize their thoughts and feelings. They can be taught to **understand** mental processes such as catastrophizing (making the very worst of a bad situation) or overgeneralizing (believing that if one bad thing happened, many more will). If your child changes their thoughts, they will be able to change their emotions. Once they realize that they are inaccurately seeing themselves as causing harm either to others or themselves, they can re-adjust their actions. Then your child will more realistically **understand** their role in whatever grief comes along.

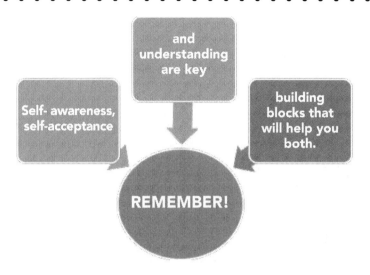

You are the most beautiful thing
I keep inside my heart.
—Unknown Author

LIFETIME SUCCESS

· · · · · · · · · · ·

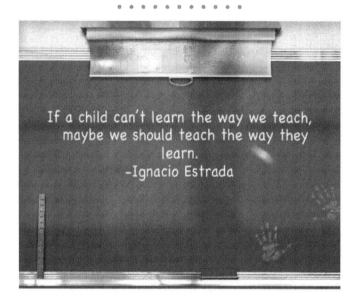

If a child can't learn the way we teach,
maybe we should teach the way they
learn.
-Ignacio Estrada

CONFLICTS

Mothers may re-live some of their own past failures and frustrations because of the difficulties and failures they see their children experience in school. Powerful feelings and painful emotions, which may also affect their parenting skills. Moms can get scared and have anxiety too! These issues frequently do not get processed properly and the discomfort continues.

In order to be a helpful mother, you must take care of yourself. You are your family's keystone. You need to be strong. Take a little "me time" for yourself.

Like any challenged family, every member will feel the tremendous impact school has on the dyslexic child. However, because dyslexia is an invisible handicap, these effects are often overlooked.

It is simple to **understand** that most non-dyslexic children are not comfortable with dyslexia, considering it as no more inconvenient than "being a bit shortsighted."

The experience of having a child who struggles with dyslexia affects mothers in a variety of ways – almost all are negative. One of the obvious is dealing with sibling rivalry. Non-dyslexic siblings often feel jealous because most of the parents' attention, time and financial support go towards the brother or sister that is struggling. **Ironically, a child with dyslexia does not want this attention!**

Going to school increases the chance that the child will act negatively towards their family and/or the achieving sibling. This means that everyone is affected. When children face problems in school, parents tend to overreact or react negatively.

Perhaps they are in denial over the existence of the dyslexia and believe that if their child would just "buckle down and work hard", they would succeed.

My Recommendations on how you and their teachers can help:
First and always, parents need to be extremely supportive, understanding and encouraging.

Second, it is important to find an area in which your child can succeed.

Finally, successful dyslexics may appear to have developed a commitment to helping others. Remember, strengths of many with dyslexia are kindness, intuitiveness, sensitivity and the ability to be vulnerable.

Teachers and parents need to offer consistent, ongoing encouragement and support. However, because most dyslexic children shy away from extra attention in the classroom, many teachers are unaware of their struggle and if they are aware, they may not know how to deal with dyslexia. Children with dyslexia are like orchids and mothers are the gardeners.

Encouragement involves at least 5 elements:
1.) Listening to feelings. Anxiety, anger and depression are daily companions.

2.) Language problems often make it difficult to express these feelings. Parents must help their child learn to talk about them.

3.) Teachers and parents must reward the child's *effort*, not just "the product." For the child with dyslexia, grades should be less important than progress.

4.) When confronting unacceptable behavior, adults must not inadvertently discourage their child. Words such as "lazy" or "incorrigible" can seriously damage a child's self-image.

5.) Help the child set realistic goals for themselves. Because some set perfectionistic and unattainable goals, by setting *attainable* goals, parents and teachers can change the cycle of failure.

Even more importantly, successes should be recognized and rejoiced in! Strengths can then become apparent and self-esteem can be developed. However, some strengths are often subtle and less obvious.

It is necessary to find ways for children to relate their interests to the demands of real life. Some children with dyslexia may deal with their own pain by reaching out to others.

Common experiences with others can help them to feel more positive and deal more effectively with pain and frustration.

Be aware that many opportunities exist in schools, homes and churches for your child to help others. One important area is peer tutoring. If one of their strengths is in math or science, being asked to tutor a classmate who is struggling can be a real boost to self-confidence.

Reciprocating as a reader for younger students with dyslexia can be a positive experience not only for them, but also family and friends as well. Observing the success of their child will help the family appreciate them and feel a sense of HOPE.

Helping your child feel better about themselves and deal effectively with their feelings is a complex task that needs great effort. But it is most rewarding.

Caring parents **must understand** the cognitive and affective problems caused by dyslexia. Design strategies that help your child find joy and success in school and personal relationships. A mother's frequent and daily reassurance is critical.

Mom, is there any good news about school?

There can be a lot of good news! Things are getting better every year. A closer investigation of the literature and interviews with young people who have dyslexia show that their feelings of being **understood** plays a vital and important role in coming to terms with dyslexia.

Self-confidence and self-esteem will improve as reading improves. Performance in school is directly related to slow reading. Early experiences at school can be confusing, but life is not a race, rather something to be enjoyed. Slow is okay. Remember, it does get better and **HOPE** is on our side.

FINANCIAL STRUGGLES

Mothers frequently send their children to special programs and extra classes such as piano, choir, scouting, music and other subjects that may help them learn better. With paid classes such as these, financial demands increase. There are also additional educational costs that often occur like tutors, assistance technology, or special writing utensils, paper or even chairs. All of this can add up very quickly and be overwhelming.

It becomes a family burden when these added expenses keep increasing. This is illustrated by one mother who has a seven-year-old child with dyslexia.

She said:
"It's financially demanding...we spend a large amount of money on private school fees...then we were told that we needed other additional materials as suggested by the doctors and educators."

Another mother agrees:
"We don't know how to help them at home so we find outside help for them...nothing is cheap in the world of dyslexia. The tuition and school fees are expensive and also entail extra travel expenses. All of these extra expenses are often more than the school fees in the end."

When a child doesn't receive the teacher's full attention and cooperation, which she needs, this can result in the delay of receiving remedial and accommodative intervention which will make the dyslexia worse.

CHALLENGES

Continuing to deny the seriousness of the challenges which come with dyslexia can cause school problems to not be appropriately treated. Children will not receive proper educational remediation and they may remain at risk for becoming another tragic statistic. You *must* anticipate and prepare for the possibilities.

Mothers who are in denial may find willing co-conspirators within the educational system. In some school districts, teachers are under a gag order by school administrators and forbidden to share their concerns about the child or to provide parents with the information necessary regarding a students' lack of progress. Other schools have limited funding and resources for special education services.

Understand that dyslexic problems are not a sign of weakness or lack of ability. Your child will have to work harder than their friends to achieve good results but with continual love and encouragement, all things can be possible.

Here is a list of some of the most important things mothers must deal with when discovering their child has dyslexia.
- Maintaining the child's self-esteem
- Helping your child start homework
- Protecting your child when dealing with professionals and therapists
- Helping with personal organization
- Dealing with peer insensitivity

- Correcting any misconceptions of dyslexia which the child may have

I strongly believe the main factor for success with a child who has dyslexia is the presence of someone who is supportive and encouraging. If you are reading this, that is probably you! Know that your support and advocacy will be the most effective thing you can do. Whether you have made mistakes along the way or not. Your child needs love. Taking care of a dyslexic child is like taking care of an orchid.

You will need to protect your child's rights to learn differently. She needs to be allowed to thrive as herself so she can be the best she can possibly imagine!

BULLYING

Mothers commonly hear from their bullied child that they feel they are stupid in school because no one really **understands** them—not their teachers and sometimes not even their parents or siblings. Your child may also tell you they thought they were stupid because someone told them so.

Experiences of bullying are commonplace, because your child seems "different". This may come from your child's inability to succeed in school in a traditional way. Bullying can affect the social dimensions at school and create anxiety, fear, embarrassment and isolation.

Bullies tend to avoid and ridicule children with differences. In general, children want to fit in with a group and mix with children like themselves. Because of this, children are unlikely to mix with those they perceive as abnormal because they are afraid it might reflect badly on them. Children with dyslexia often end up isolated and with no friends.

Being humiliated in one class or area in school can have a cascading effect on your child. Even when the teacher is helpful, a child with dyslexia will still be reeling and calming down from the last humiliating experience.

In such a challenging and hostile environment, dyslexics know that they can either sink or swim. 'Sinking' comes from believing what everyone else is saying—that they are worthless and need to withdraw as a form of protection.

"Swimming" is another means to gain popularity, e.g., being the class clown, physically attacking anyone who tries to humiliate them or developing other skills of note – sports, drama, crafts or alternative hobbies.

The failure to recognize bullying at school causes children great frustration, fear and anger. Additionally, there can be humiliation by peers when they are unable to read aloud in class or have work handed back by teachers with red marks all over it. In most cases, extreme defenses must be developed in advance.

Typically, other children can and will be cruel.

Have trouble reading facial expressions and body language that should be telling the, "Danger, this person intends to harm you."

Have trouble reading social cues, especially the cues that tell them when someone is saying one thing but means another.

Are an easy mark for "practical jokes" because they tend to be literal-minded.

Are often scoalized out of saying no, even when they are uncomfortable with something.

May not have the language abilities to stand up for themselves under duress.

Tend to care less about social conventions than other people so they make easy targets for mockery based on what's socially "in" or "popular".

Often don't have a group of friends to shelter, defend or stand up for them.

Can be easy to provoke making them a reactive target.

May be more likely than others to believe that they've brought harassment on themselves due to low self-esteem, or being conditioned to think they're weird, defective or damaged.

We know it is possible that bullying can occur and may result in sadness! Prepare and learn how to deal with these people. First, we need to be **understood**. Give it a try and be patient.

Boosting self-esteem is seen by some as the "social vaccine" to help deal with bullying, social and emotional challenges. This is where dyslexics are treated fairly, justly and with respect. However, boosting self-esteem by removing competition so no one fails, or praising when no praise is warranted, **is not going to help**.

> Anything that annoys you is teaching you patience. Anyone who abondons you is teaching you how to stand up on your own two feet. Anything that angers you is teaching you forgiveness and compassion. Anything that has power over you is teaching you how to take your power back. Anything you can't control is teaching you how to let go.
>
> —Jackson

Unfortunately, most interactions for a child with dyslexia involve not just a few events, but many. With sequencing and memory problems, they may relate a different sequence of events each time they tell the story. Teachers, parents and psychologists may conclude that the child is psychotic or a pathological liar.

Their inconsistencies produce serious challenges. There is a large variation in abilities. Although everyone has strengths and weaknesses, the *weaknesses of a child with dyslexia are great*. Increasing life experiences helps to discover strengths.

Dyslexics may perform erratically within tasks. Errors are often inconsistent and their **performance can vary from day** to day. On some days, reading may come easily.

Your child may be physically and socially immature compared to their peers. This can lead to a poor self-image and less peer acceptance.

Your child's social immaturity may make them feel awkward in social situations.

Your child may have difficulty reading social cues. They may be oblivious to the amount of personal distance necessary in social interactions or be insenstive to other people's body language.

Your child often experiences oral language dysfunction. They may have trouble finding the right words or may stammer or pause before answering direct questions. This puts them at a disadvantage as they enter adolescence when language becomes more central to their relationships with peers.

Your child may often experience two major difficulties:

1.) It will take longer to learn from mistakes.

2.) If anyone questions them as to what may have happened, they may seem to be lying.

However, other days they may barely be able to write their own name. This inconsistency is extremely confusing—not only to the dyslexic, but also to the mothers. Remember loving kindness.

ANGER

Typically, mothers may also feel frightened, helpless, i solated and even out of control. To assert some sense of control, mothers may attempt to assign blame for their child's problems to school personnel, the child, their partner, themselves, or on luck or fate. Instead, it's a good idea to step back and re-evaluate the issues. Intense feelings must find an outlet.

> The key words to keep repeating are: *Awareness, Acceptance, Analysis* and development of an *Action* plan.

To avoid feelings of guilt and sadness, mothers may externalize their emotions by blaming someone else for the problems their children are experiencing. Sometimes this blame may be warranted. When mothers believe they have been betrayed by the teachers in whom they placed their trust, their anger and sense of personal outrage can be intense.

Anger can often lead to depression, maternal issues, divorce and drug dependency. Again, strong advocacy is **imperative**. Even if it is unfamiliar and difficult, self-awareness plus determination and persistence can be omnipotent, and resolve problems once thought unsolvable, or better yet, stop a problem before it starts.

Parents who obsess about the transgressions caused by the school system often *"burn out"* **without achieving anything that is of true value to your child!!**

Being angry about the hard choices and sacrifices that must be made is okay. However, express your concerns to the teachers or the school itself, not to each other.

"Allowing a student with a hidden disability (ADHD, dyslexia, dysgraphia…) to struggle academically when all that is needed for success are appropriate accommodations and explicit instruction is no different than failing to provide a ramp for a person in a wheelchair."

—Professor Samuel Stein

• •

SHAME

School shame can fuel anger which can bring fear, even for an adult. Some children direct their anger outward, while others focus it inward. Each moment of anger will provide a powerful distraction from the experience of shame and the feelings that accompany it.

Shame, like guilt and embarrassment, involves negatively judging oneself when you believe you have failed to live up to either your own or others' standards.

Guilt and Shame

Recall a time when you experienced shame, perhaps in school. Was it a reaction to being judged by others or yourself? You most likely experienced intense discomfort, feelings of inadequacy and unworthness, and the desire to hide. Crying is common and you probably felt anger toward those who brought on these feelings. Your child feels the same way.

School shame can be paralyzing and may remain with your child forever. When severe, it can form the basis through which all evaluation is viewed.

Words to express the emotion of shame:

Insecure

Worthless

Stupid

Foolish

Silly

Inadequate

Simply less than

Everyone experiences guilt and shame at some time in their life. Not everyone feels overwhelmed. Some researchers suggest that shame in dyslexics comes about from repeated criticism. Consequently, it can close the child off from accepting any form of positive regard from others or themselves.

Mothers must be on the lookout for school shame. It can undermine dyslexics from being fully present with others and with themselves. This makes perfect sense. It takes a lot of energy to protect themselves against the vulnerability to feel shame. **Most importantly, difficulty with shame leaves them prone to anger** – anger that results when natural desires for love, connection and validation are inhibited by the impenetrable barrier of shame.

> For a child with dyslexia, shame may also be caused by the failure of their efforts, achievements or ideas.
> These may be conveyed in repeated statements such as:
> *"Why are you doing it that way?"*
> *"What were you thinking?*
> *"That won't work"*, or more directly
> *"No matter how much you try, you won't be as good as others."*

School shame may also arise as an outcome of physical, sexual or emotional abuse. A child may initially feel puzzled and then angry when a teacher neglects them, whether emotionally or physically. When neglected, the lack of sufficient parental availability and presence can be interpreted by a child to mean, "I'm not worthy of love and attention."

When your child is heavily dependent on you, it is important to help them realize that you cannot be with them at all times, or in all situations. They may become fearful when they make you angry and quickly experience shame when they do something to upset you.

This kind of fear, whether based in reality or not, can lead to shame regarding anger and, worse yet, minimization or denial of deep hurt—including sadness, betrayal and powerlessness. A child with dyslexia needs to learn to conclude that mom would not do anything to harm or neglect them.

Avoiding shame may become a lifetime pursuit. Anger may become the go-to response in reaction to the slightest arousal of shame or thoughts and feelings that might trigger it.

Be alert that it is possible a child may start using alcohol or drugs as a form of self-medication to reduce shame.

Never judge a student by the opinion of other teachers.
Every child deserves a fresh start.

CONFUSION

- Why do I have to be faced each day with the simple task of learning to read when everyone else can do it without struggle?

- Do any of the people in my life understand how it feels to be dyslexic and how to help?

- If learning to read and spell is so important, what *effect* does my inability have on my future?

- Is there really a good "one solution fits all" approach to reading?

- What are the long-term effects of slipping through the cracks and not being properly diagnosed?

On the positive side, difficulty with reading is much less of a problem than being unable to form relationships.

SELF-ESTEEM

School is the **primary source** of negative emotions, social experiences and low self-esteem for many children with dyslexia. This is most probably because teachers and peers do not fully **understand** all of the other issues which accompany dyslexia. Early school experiences can create a collection of frightening, hurtful or humiliating experiences that leave very bad memories and scars.

Self-esteem, like self-concept and other similar concepts starting with "self," is concerned with overall personal awareness of one's own self-worth. "Self-esteem" encompasses beliefs about a person, e.g. I am confident, I am worthy.

Self-esteem is the sum of all individual successes so far, divided by pretentions of what one believes he or she ought to have achieved.

To increase self-esteem, success needs to be gained, failure avoided and current self-esteem maintained. Adopting less ambitious goals (or realistic goals) will increase the frequency of success.

In my life, I have observed that self-esteem is competence-orientated, but with the ability to change or develop. Worthiness should be brought into the debate. Dyslexics must learn that self-esteem is the ability to judge oneself.

After school, a **child needs downtime**: time to reconnect with mom, rest, start a new activity, maybe have some private time—anything that is opposite school. Success in these areas will improve self-esteem.

> Parents need to realize that self-esteem is
> important to their child's identity and awareness.
> Having high or low levels will influence their
> attitude towards life. Self-esteem is the status
> of their competence in dealing with the challenges of living
> in a worthwhile way over time.
> Thus, self-esteem is a dynamic living phenomenon

You could compare self-esteem with a coral reef, which can't be seen growing and yet it is a dynamic, living organism on which so many other living things (like the rest of the moving emotional parts of ourselves) are dependent on for their own life.

I want parents to never forget that self-esteem is an important predictor of academic and other achievements. **A child's belief in their self will greatly affect their abilities,** like a self-

• •

fulfilling prophecy. **If you believe you will do well, there is a good chance you will!** Studies with teachers have found that if the teacher believes a student will do well, they probably will and vice-versa. Students will fail or struggle **if the teacher believes that will happen.**

Dyslexics always worry about how other children and adults view them. This may show by way of children making more negative comparisons between themselves and others, putting themselves down, etc. They may express more doubts about their ability or competence. These children need to receive high levels of reassurance, feedback and most of all love and **understanding.**

> Successful children with dyslexia
> learn to be AWARE of their dyslexia.

Common reactions that I have observed:

☀ "I feel stupid."

☀ "I feel different."

☀ "I am never picked to do cool things, because I can't read or remember things like everyone else."

☀ "I am not being understood" – confusing dyslexic with stupid

☀ "I feel embarrassed"

A Mother's Personal Experience:

Another challenge in raising a child with dyslexia is related to issues at school. This is illustrated by one mother. She stressed:

"My son always has a traumatic response to reading; maybe because his teacher doesn't know and doesn't understand how to handle a child with dyslexia. They might talk too loud-

ly to my son. It affects my son so that he refuses to read at all, and it is difficult for me to encourage him to read."

A 35-year-old full-time housewife said:

"I was not happy with the way the teacher treated her. My daughter said that the teacher was impatient and beat her. I went to school and found out that yes, it is true that the teacher beats my child's hands because the teacher thought that she was being a lazy writer...So she moved to another class...no complaints...I checked...the teacher completely ignored her... And they never told me anything...Whenever I asked, they said that my child was okay, even when I noticed that my child has a problem and gets angry at them...only then did they confess to me that my child has a problem."

> Live So That When Your Children Think Of Fairness, Caring, And Integrity, They Think Of You.
> —The Fresh Quotes

ACTING-OUT

I want to share with you my experience with behavioral characteristics:

Attention-Seeking

Dyslexics frequently seek higher levels of attention, e.g. seeking for help more often, talking and laughing with others, shouting out answers and not taking turns.

Clowning

Dyslexics may seek a role as the class joker and through that, obtain positive feedback from peers.

Aggression

Dyslexics may experience higher levels of failure and may also have poor relationship skills. They may resort to aggressive behavior, especially when frustrated or feeling threatened by a task.

Withdrawal

Dyslexics may adopt a strategy of withdrawal or "disappearing" in order to avoid the stress of experiencing failure.

A child may fear that due to their academic performance, they will lose your support and love.

Research teaches that there is a strong and positive connection between self-esteem and school achievement. **The greater the self-esteem**, the easier it is to learn and retain information. The same applies to the ability to handle difficult situations later in life.

Difficult situations:
- Prejudice
- Failure
- Solitude
- Violence

Dyslexia often centers on the inability of the child to meet expectations! Parents and teachers may see a bright, enthusiastic child who is not learning to read and write.

Time and again, parents hear the following: "You have a bright child; if only they would try harder." Ironically, no one knows the truth of how hard your child really is trying! Much of dyslexia is an emotional experience.

Dyslexia, almost by definition, means that the individual will be slow and make some "careless" or "stupid" mistakes. This is extremely frustrating, because it makes the child feel chronically inadequate.

SELF-IMAGE

Self-image is extremely vulnerable to frustration and anxiety. During the first years of school, the conflicts between a positive self-image and feelings of inferiority must be resolved. If success is to happen in school, the child must develop positive feelings about themselves and believe that they can succeed in life. This is frequently absent among dyslexics. These feelings will continue throughout their lives.

> Dyslexia can't be cured because it's not a disease.
> **Dyslexics aren't broken so they can't be fixed.**
> Their brains are just different.
> —Ben Foss

Lack of self-confidence shows itself in everything the dyslexic does. Whether their difficulties have been noticed and given a label, they will know very well that they are inadequate in several ways.

Researchers have learned that when *non-dyslexic* learners succeed, they credit their own efforts for their success. When dyslexics fail, they tell themselves to try harder. However, when they succeed, they are likely to attribute this success to luck.

Research suggests that feelings of inferiority may develop by the age of four. And after this age, it becomes much more difficult to help develop a positive self-image.

To be beautiful means to
be yourself.

You need to accept yourself.
—Thich Nhat Hanh

Dyslexics fear being assigned a task that they know they won't be able to achieve. Petrified! This is an experience many dyslexic children carry over from childhood. There is a slowness in developing skills and a feeling of not performing very well. This is a daily event in their minds.

Give your child tasks they can do successfully.
It really does make a difference!

If your child likes books, tell them success stories about dyslexic authors. If they like sports, then tell them about sports figures. Tell them about scientists, artists or maybe a family member. Some interests can be encouraged successfully. Creativity is a common asset.

Remind them that they aren't the only ones with dyslexia (10% - 20% of the population have it). This gives them reassurance that other people learn the same way they do. Patience and determination are omnipotent.

Dyslexics experience difficulties through developmental stages, such as walking, talking, tying shoelaces, telling time, reading and writing. Early on they develop a sense of inadequacy.

Remember the 4 A's. These DO work.
Reassurance creates strength!

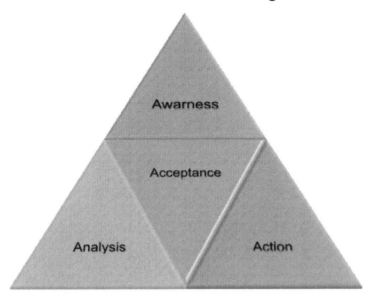

Your reassurance may be a necessary daily event. It does work! It seems to me that this reassurance always falls on a mother's shoulders. It's hard for mothers to be strong 24/7. **Moms need to develop their own coping mechanism.** With all of these problems, difficulties, perceived inefficiencies and traumas, it is very challenging for a mother to hold onto her self-perception of worth. She may tend to react in one of two ways: either becoming withdrawn or defensive or becoming bad-tempered and aggressive.

> It is never easy for a mother!
> Only another mom who cares for a dyslexic childcan truly understand the emotional, mental and physical demands.

Some mothers may try to hide their lack of confidence to help their child behind an aggressive exterior. They may become isolated and feel apprehensive! **It may lead to isolation, often daily.**

When a mother's lack of confidence results in aggressive or defensive behavior, they feel trapped in a fluctuating pattern of interaction, reaction, defense and aggression, isolation and distress.

> TIP:
> Negative emotions can be overcome
> By both managing the effects of dyslexia
> And teaching positive coping
> Strategies or mindfulness.

Negative emotions have been associated with a decrease in reading, social and emotional skills, as well as increasing anxiety. It is important for mothers to **understand** and discuss the importance of developing positive coping strategies early, before maladaptive coping patterns are established. **Negative feelings can cause negative effects on reading skills.** Read that last sentence three (3) times a day.

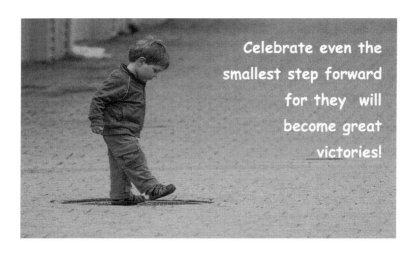

Celebrate even the smallest step forward for they will become great victories!

SCHOOL REINFORCEMENTS

. . . .

"There comes a moment when you
realize that what you're advocating
for is more than just
accommodations. You're really
advocating for someone's quality of lie.
That's the moment you realize...

YOU WON'T GIVE UP!"

—Kellie Henkel

ENCOURAGEMENT
Mom, here are some great ideas:

- Reward effort, not the finished product.
- Avoid using labels like "lazy" or "stubborn."
- Help set realistic goals—learning takes longer, but can be achieved.
- Implement effective accommodations.

Mothers' Stress and Coping Strategies:

■ Mothers of children affected by dyslexia feel a much higher level of in all parental stresses.

■ Mothers of children with dyslexia report a significantly higher rate of emotion-oriented and avoidance-oriented coping styles than mothers of typical-developing children.

• •

■ There is a lower representation of task-oriented coping style in mothers of a dyslexic child in comparison to mothers of typical children.

Dealing with your child's dyslexia is one of life's greatest challenges for mothers. One of the burdens carried by mothers of dyslexic children is knowing the importance of improving **family understanding**, **acceptance** and the clinical management of dyslexia.

When someone else's child has dyslexia, it's a challenge. When your child has dyslexia, it's a problem.

Social dysfunction can be caused by several variables, which may contribute to academic problems:
- Congenital deficits
- Neuropathological abnormalities
- Language disorders
- Memory impairment
- Cognition delays
- Preterm birth

I repeat, maternal coping skills and parents' perceptions of their child's issues require daily reassurance. These skills are based on information that the parents were either provided, actively sought out from professionals, or from informal sources after receiving their child's diagnosis. The way the parents process and cope with their knowledge of their child's illness will enhance their ability to instill **HOPE**.

> As maternal knowledge grows, a developed
> skill improvement will follow.
> Maternal acceptance, analysis and
> action plans will lead to understanding
> and an overall improvement for the child.
> Again, it is easy to say, but difficult to do.

In general, learning difficulties and scholastic problems tend to impact negatively on parenting quality due to the high level of stress making a mother's reassurance difficult.

Dyslexics with learning disabilities tend to present lower self-concept, more anxiety and lower peer acceptance. As a result, your maternal stress will make the child less successful.

Mothers may initially respond to the diagnosis with denial and ambivalence about their child's disability. This may create unrealistic maternal expectations for their child's academic performance and thus add to more family stress.

Dyslexia
is a
connection
problem.

Development of new circuits or Neuroplasticity, can lead to improvement. Reassurance is critically important and very helpful.

Dyslexics may have sensory perception disorder and often ADD. This causes a dramatic increased and persistent level of frustration and dissatisfaction. In fact, mothers who report high levels of stress from these life events **appear to be more controlling**, abusive and punitive than mothers who have lower levels of stress!

The answer is self-awareness and self-acceptance. These are key foundations for every mom. Controlling emotions requires changing thoughts.

The additional maternal stress associated with raising a child with dyslexia may adversely affect the child in several ways: insecure attachments, low family cohesion, and an increase in internalizing and externalizing behavior (ex: anger, fear, worry, etc.)

> Children with dyslexia are **needier** and **more dependent** on others and often trail their peers in terms of their level of independence.

This dependence will pre-dispose parents to higher levels of stress. In particular, mothers of dyslexic children present higher rates of emotion-oriented and avoidance-oriented coping styles.

These include higher rates of self-oriented reactions (i.e., emotional responses, self-preoccupation and fantasizing). Proper reassurance helps moms to be self-aware and self-accepting.

SELF-ADVOCACY

A person with dyslexia who understands their diagnosis can then be taught to advocate for themselves. This means they can tell teachers, friends or any other leaders what their needs are up front. They no longer need to wait until a situation has gotten out of control before beginning the conversation.

Studies have shown that children who are anxious have trouble learning. I cannot over emphasize this key point. If your child is anxious about schoolwork, it may be best to back off the academics for some time. I have noticed that there is a lot of freedom in homeschooling.

I recommend that both of you take a break. This may seem counterintuitive, especially if your child is already "behind" their peers who are traditional learners. A child with dyslexia fatigues, has more frustration, and more down days. Moms need to remember this and **understand** their child.

Taking a break doesn't mean the learning stops. Taking a break can simply mean stepping away from the books for some real-life learning. Go to the beach, museums, conferences, expos or anything that your child likes. Use these opportunities for learning. Read, research and learn together. Show them that **learning can be fun and rewarding** and they will gradually come around. I have always said I learned more after school than in the classroom!

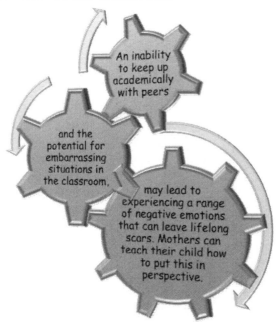

An inability to keep up academically with peers

and the potential for embarrassing situations in the classroom,

may lead to experiencing a range of negative emotions that can leave lifelong scars. Mothers can teach their child how to put this in perspective.

SOCIAL AND EMOTIONAL
Mom, what exactly is this SEL stuff?

Social and Emotional Learning (SEL) has been defined as systematic instruction designed to teach students social and emotional skills – both as a preventive measure and as an early intervention for mental health problems from pre-K to 12th grade.

My experience has observed that SEL programs are primarily used as interventions in schools to help support five core social-emotional competencies:

1. Self-Management
2. Social Awareness
3. Relationship Skills
4. Self-Awareness
5. Responsible Decision-Making

Self-management refers to the ability to regulate behaviors and emotions to achieve goals. Social awareness involves understanding and empathizing with others.

In reading dyslexia literature, I have concluded that relationship skills include:

- The ability to cooperate
- Manage conflict
- Develop social and emotional relationships

Self-awareness refers to the ability to identify personal emotions, as well as strengths and challenges. Responsible decision-making involves making ethical, constructive decisions about personal and social behavior and interactions.

The premise of SEL programs is that these skills must be taught just like other subjects in school. *These skills are critical to the emotional, behavioral and academic success, and health of the child with dyslexia.*

One of the first steps in SEL is how to get things done (executive functioning). So, what if your child doesn't complete a job the same day they started? They can sometimes just roll it over to the next day. If that's not possible, perhaps it can be rescheduled to another time.

Personally, I have developed what I call my "A list, B list and C list" in order to prioritize issues. I have always prepared the night before by writing my agenda for the next day. Think "Sticky Notes".

K-12 students with dyslexia in SEL programs have significantly improved social and emotional skills, behaviors and attitudes. Of note, is that students in SEL groups also demonstrate academic performance gains, with a significant gain in achievement.

> "There needs to be a lot more emphasis on what a child CAN do, instead of what he cannot do."
> —Dr. Temple Grandi

A child that participates in **SEL programs can develop skills** such as:
SEL can teach your child the power of learning optimism and *HOPEfulness* as a treatment for pessimism and helplessness. These programs can be a keystone.

Once your child enters school, SEL will help them to learn skills needed to deal with failure and to help them be successful and may allow your child to **understand** why they fail. Most importantly, SEL can help your child change **failure into success.**

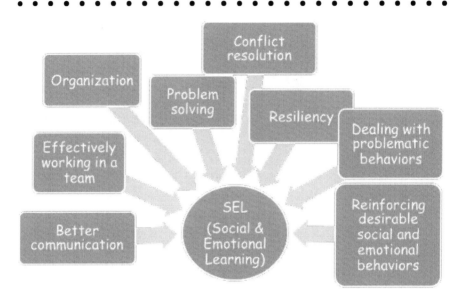

Parents who cushion their child from failure are doing them a disservice. This holds them back from normal development. It weakens them just as if they had been belittled, humiliated and physically threatened at every turn.

Children need to learn balance. I am concerned that parents may not be aware or even accept this important concept.

The feel-good self-esteem movement, which avoids children failing in tasks by over-simplifying curriculum or tests cheapens success and **may produce a generation of very expensive failures.**

A child may fear that due to their academic performance, they will lose your support and love.

Through SEL they will come to learn the value of balance in their lives.

RESILIENCE TO FAILURE

In the case of a dyslexic student, it may be hard to develop resilience to failure. Constant and repeated failure is common in school-aged dyslexics. A child with dyslexia may tend to give up, choose to avoid difficult to spell words, hide in class, or avoid the most difficult and challenging tasks. Be on guard for what might be subtle changes in behavior which may lead to becoming an "invisible student."

Many teachers in mainstream education have large numbers of students and are relieved to have quiet ones. But quiet students in most cases are those who are avoiding the teacher's radar. Intelligent students without dyslexia are the ones who challenge the teacher and ask questions. Only the students who stay on the teacher's radar will get the help they need. A child with dyslexia likes to be the "invisible student."

Children are made readers
on the laps of their parents!

Parents can sometimes be to blame because they use similar avoidance techniques themselves. They want their children to do well in homework tasks, so they may do more than just answer their child's questions. Parents may go as far as completing the homework for them. However, if the child were to do their own homework and get it wrong, then the teacher would know that extra help is needed.

If your child's homework is always correct, the teacher will not be concerned that there may be a serious problem. If the homework is correct, but the student is unable to do the tasks themselves in school, the teacher will conclude that they are lazy or not paying attention. There is a mis-match from the homework to the classroom work. This could further exacerbate an already difficult problem for the child in school.

> *Parents should allow their children to fail in homework tasks, as only this will inform teachers that extra help is needed.*

The difference between a typical student and a dyslexic student is that the dyslexic student has failed more times than the typical student has even tried. To gain real mastery, one needs to first experience failure and then overcome it after several attempts. If mastery is gained the first time around, then the necessary and vital building blocks are left out.

Two Keys to Resistance Failure:
1. Work the hardest on keeping your child's self-esteem as high as possible. Focus on the things they get right and the things they like to do. That will give them more incentive to do the things they struggle with.

2. Find positive support – whatever it takes, even if it means homeschooling. Many children in the school system are made fun of simply because they think differently. Your child must **understand** that seeing everything differently is an advantage, not a disadvantage.

> At the end of the day, remind yourself that you did the best you could today, and that is good enough.

What is Frustration?
Frustration is what schools may often give to mom.

Without question, all schools and all teachers should meet the needs of individual students. Teachers must also meet the demands placed on them by school management, budgets and the educational system. These demands are often based on principles relating to accountability and results.

In my experience being an advocate can present a great difficulty for mothers, schools and teachers. Dads rarely get involved. Progress made by those with dyslexia is **not always easily measured** and certainly not by conventional means.

For some children with dyslexia, merely attending school can be a measure of success. But schools may not record this as progress and instead focus on progress of attainments such as reading, spelling and writing.

Teachers usually have no training in dyslexia. Rarely can they make a diagnosis or have the time necessary to find out what is wrong.

Remember children with dyslexia may not make significant progress in school – at least not in the short term. This may lead to a lot of frustration on the part of mothers. This lack of significant progress clearly highlights the different agendas between home and school. This underlines the importance of effective and shared communication. Advocacy is demanding, but is imperative! The teachers need to know who you are and how very connected you are.

TRUST

Not all teachers, in fact, very few are familiar with dyslexia. It can sometimes be difficult for parents to place their trust in a system that may not even recognize dyslexia. But this is exactly what they must do! Parents have a critical role to play in providing information on dyslexia to schools. It does not need to be the other way around. Remember trust, but verify!

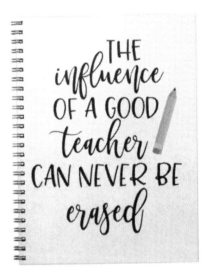

BALANCED STRESS

Mothers often ask how they can balance the stress their child experiences in schoolwork with life at home. This is difficult because the **stress that is experienced at school can often spill over into home life,** especially since potential stresses, such as homework, can take up an unduly amount of time. Homework can overcome a family. **Accommodations are critical.** Homework must be limited to time – **NOT quantity.** Do not give into the school on this point!

> **TIP**
> Like all evenings, time at home should include fun, or at least include some free time. It rarely happens! This may be difficult to achieve without making light of the work that must be done. Fun family-oriented activities or games can provide learning strategies, develop language skills and boost self-esteem. These are usually limited to the weekends.

EMOTIONAL ASPECTS

If a child is failing in literacy or finds some aspects of learning challenging, mothers will be affected by this emotionally! It is important that you address this so that you may be able to prevent it.

There are several ways of helping your child maintain and boost their self-esteem. One of the most obvious and effective ways is to ensure that some success is achieved and genuine praise is given from you, family members, friends and *themselves*.

Several mothers have told me that the following can be useful for **developing self-esteem** in children:
- Paired reading
- Mind-mapping, including software mapping
- Memory games
- Opportunities to use verbal skills
- Focusing on discussions about areas of success

The very important role mothers can play in helping their child deal with difficulties is of far-reaching importance and not easy to accomplish. Mothers are the first "port of call" and probably the last, particularly in kindergarten and the early years. It is so important for mothers to instill HOPE whenever they can.

Communication at this level has the potential to really help your child. Minimizing anxieties and maximizing parental skills, as well as assisting in the identification of the difficulties associated with dyslexia is frequently overwhelming. There should be an attempt to anticipate and plan ahead to implement these skills.

One of the key aspects is communication, particularly communication with the school. It is important, despite the anxieties and the difficulties faced by moms themselves. Positive developments in the schools' awareness of and support for those with dyslexia should be acknowledged by the parents, so that the schools will continue in their efforts.

The school should have adequate support systems and facilities available. No parent of a child with dyslexia should ever feel isolated by the school. This is one of moms' greatest problems and it requires much persistence, determination, self-awareness, acceptance and self-advocacy. It seems to me that this is a constant problem that must be constantly attended to.

> Motherhood always includes difficult periods.
> There are times when mothers feel concerned
> and confused. Sleepless nights result when
> mothers worry about how well they are fulfilling
> their responsibilities to their children.

A friend and mother I recently met with said this to me:
"Raising a dyslexic child ups the ante. Meeting the complex needs of your child with dyslexia can be extraordinarily difficult, frustrating, emotionally draining and expensive! You

will experience worry, sadness, fear, guilt, helplessness, anger, confusion, disappointment and more worry."

> Mothers of dyslexic children need to understand one crucial fact "only by obtaining an appropriate education will my child have a real opportunity to lead a fulfilling, productive life." Unfortunately, statistics regarding the outcomes of special education programs will not alleviate many concerns.

The intense emotions experienced by mothers often become their "Achilles heel" as they attempt to obtain an appropriate education for their child. When the local school system *fails* to provide their child with that critical "special" educational experience, or offers "too little too late," many parents are shocked and angry. A maternal experience I observed:

"One of the great tragedies of parental disillusionment is that even if we finally find a good education program, we know that our child can be damaged by people within the school system. We don't know how severe or enduring the damage will be. The feelings of betrayal are often so strong and bitter that there will never be any trust by the parents."

Please remember to tell me:
You do not have a disorder, or a disability.
You have a different learning style!

 Be organized and write things down. Sticky notes are awesome! Thoughts can be just as random as words and letters are constantly getting jumbled. However, when the thoughts are written and lists are made, it is much easier to see what needs to be done. The iCloud calendar, MacBook, PC, phone or a notebook are all different ways to keep track.

 Estimate the amount of time it will take to complete each task. I suggest writing the time next to the task on their list or block out a period of time on the calendar. The importance of this step is to see what is possible and what is not possible to get done within a specific period of time.

 Set priorities. Put a star beside the items that must be done that day and a √checkmark by the things that can be put off. This step shows the different levels of importance in priorities.

 Assign a specific time on the schedule to start the task. At this point, have the tasks organized and prioritized for whatever period of time it will take to complete the list.

These tips will help kids to stay focused throughout the day. It will also help any unrecognized ADD.

> You can't cure dyslexia,
> because it's not a disease.
> Dyslexics aren't broken,
> so you can't fix them.
> Our brains are just different!!
>
> —Ben Foss

 What does Dr. O'Leary recommend?

■ Encourage your child to believe they do have some control over their learning.

■ Avoid giving ability-based attributions when talking, e.g. "You are clever" could be replaced by "You worked hard."

■ When a task has proved difficult, help explain to your child the difficulty by saying that success requires persistence, patience and determination.

■ Challenge any unhelpful reason which was given for success or failure. Suggest an alternative, e.g. "I can't do physics. I'm HOPEless at it" and challenge it by saying, "No, everybody finds the work they are doing hard. It's not that they are HOPEless. It will just take more practice and explanation."

■ Sometimes a teacher can help your child by taking responsibility for a task difficulty by saying things like, "No, it's not that you are no good at this. Maybe I just didn't explain it well enough. Maybe I made the questions too hard."

HOMEWORK

A major emotional roadblock is usually homework. I have heard that normal one hour of homework can take a dyslexic child over two hours! This is very often a source of **great stress and frustration** for both mom and student. It has great potential for raising levels of anxiety.

For a school-age child, the parent may only see them during weekdays for a few hours. Half an hour to one hour (or even more in some cases) of this time may be normally spent doing homework.

Frequently, children with dyslexia require two hours to do homework. Remember, accommodations are necessary, sometimes even mandatory.

If stress runs high during this time, you may both be experiencing negative emotions. A sensitive and vulnerable child may worry unduly about how their own reading difficulties and the extra stress and time demands it requires affects their parents' thoughts and feelings about them.

Parents may need help or guidance in how to approach reading at home. There needs to be a way that does not worsen the difficulties, increase anxiety or damage the parent/child relationship. This means finding a way to read together that avoids making errors, which often are the source of the emotional stress. This often sounds and feels overwhelming. It is as if you are asked to be a **SUPER MOM**.

> **Never Give Up. Things Do Get Better!**

Maternal Personal Experiences:
Most mothers express that there are often serious time constraints in managing their dyslexic children. At the same time, children with dyslexia need extra time and assistance to finish their homework.

A friend of a dyslexic child once told me that:
"Time is always a big challenge. After sending my child to one school, I learned that I needed to send her to a different one. All these issues were very difficult for me, but I had to endure it."

Another mother stated:
"Sometimes I teach my child. But, when I'm at home, there are only a few hours left before he goes to bed. We need more time to do his homework because he does not understand. During weekends, I try to find time to sit with him. I have to be very patient. I do get frequently overwhelmed and frustrated. So, I stop and reflect on HOPE."

Most parents do not know how to teach their children in the correct way. As illustrated by a mother:
"We don't know how to teach him...I don't know what else that I can do to help my son...I just have to tolerate whatever problems he creates."

When you...
Cut it for me,
Write it for me,
Open it for me,
Set it up for me,
Draw it for me,
All I learn is that you do it better than me.

—Orton Gillingham Online Academy

INTERVENTION STRATEGIES

There is a wide range of possible intervention strategies for mothers to use. The following is a small set of possible ones. They target some of the most common facets of the emotional consequences of dyslexic difficulties.

Teacher-Pupil Relationship

Possibly the most important aspect of a successful approach to helping your child will be the quality of the relationship between the teacher, the parent and the child. This needs to be founded on **understanding and empathy**.

> ### REMEMBER
> Students always place more importance on a teacher's personal characteristics than on the educational material. They can't handle teachers who shout, get angry, rush them or don't encourage them.

After analyzing comments from dyslexic children about what they found difficult or positive in class, I heard a mom say:

"It is interesting that the underlying theme is the emotional climate in the classroom, rather than any specific techniques or special methodology. They want calmness and security, and the feeling that teachers might actually like them...'"

It frequently may be that teachers need to be taught to make extra effort to communicate these things! Their usual way of teaching may not be perceived as being supportive enough. This is a very "touchy" situation. You must be gentle and strong at the same time.

Teachers need to be aware of just how important tone of voice, facial expressions and body language can be to a child with dyslexia. These skills cannot be taken for granted with pupils who are highly sensitive to success and failure. Each learning experience represents a significant extension of trust. This **must** be recognized by the classroom teacher.

Teachers of dyslexic children in particular need to realize that dyslexics need supportiveness, friendliness and nurture to properly learn. These can all be communicated by tone of voice (soft, relaxed, calm) and warm and gentle eye contact (not staring or avoiding focus). Frequent encouragement and supportive comments are necessary. Dyslexic students are like orchids.

The most precious jewels you'll ever have around your neck are the arms of your children.

The hardest part of being a parent is watching your child go through something tough and not being able to fix it for them.

SUPPORT FOR MOM

. . . .

Grief is like the ocean;
Waves ebbing and flowing.
Sometimes the water is calm, and
sometimes it is overwhelming.
All we can learn to do is swim.

—Vicki Harrison

LOSS OF THE PERFECT CHILD

As an obstetrician for 41 years, I am very aware of this maternal experience. When children enter mothers' lives there is excitement, anticipation and joy. Moms have high HOPES and great expectations for their child. How do they process the new reality that this much-loved child has a serious "life challenge"? Or that this difficulty may negatively affect the child's ability to live a productive, satisfying and independent life?

Mothers are at an enormous disadvantage when they discover that their child has dyslexia; they are in shock and they grieve. They don't know that there are laws. They don't know about the IDEA*. They don't know that their child has any rights.

Mothers just trust for the first couple of years. Then something happens that causes them to become a little suspicious and they begin to investigate things.

* See Stepping Stone #8

Maternal mourning is a natural, necessary and healthy process that begins when you learn that your child has dyslexia. If not handled appropriately, the mourning process will continue for years. Sadness is a normal part of the mourning process, but improves over time.

It is normal for mothers to feel some guilt, sadness, anger and regret which often merge into a painful tangle of emotions. A mother's feelings of guilt about her own lack of knowledge of disabilities and lack of self-confidence, combined with a pattern of conflict avoidance can all combine to make her an ineffective advocate for her child.

My observations are that some parents try to avoid experiencing feelings of sadness and regret, preferring to remain sad. It can, however, be helpful to mourn the loss of HOPE for a "perfect child." Mourning the loss is not the same as rejecting your child, or finding them less worthy of your love. Instead, it is part of the process of acceptance and resolution. This can free you to move on.

Because the mourning process may involve intense painful emotions, many parents try to avoid it by minimizing or denying their feelings. Other moms get "stuck" in one phase and fail to complete the process. **Awareness and acceptance are the first key steps**.

Like people who see themselves as "victims" of divorce, mothers can remain angry, bitter, guilty or depressed for years or for life. They can become mired in negative emotions, and thus accomplish little of value for their child.

Remember, you must not let this happen to you. Stay connected and always have a good friend, if possible. Try to identify with a successful adult dyslexic. Sharing is very therapeutic.

Failure to deal with reality, remain in denial and refuse to acknowledge that their child's problems are serious will cause other problems and keep their child from receiving necessary educational services.

> Come to terms with the loss and mourn the hopes and dreams that may never be realized. In common with other major losses, mourning encompasses predictable emotional stages.

Typically, parents move back and forth between these stages, especially in the early months and years following their child's diagnosis.

Acceptance, persistence, determination and understanding are simple to say, but can be overwhelming and very difficult to achieve. Careers are frequently disrupted. Family expenses change radically. Family income can be severely reduced leading to significant distress at home.

Mothers might say, "I don't believe it." They may try to convince themselves that their child is just a late bloomer. However, many children with dyslexia have had to repeat grades. But it's okay! Slower is good; slower works. Summer school and repeating may frequently make good sense. Just don't give up.

GRATITUDE

I have met moms who say that gratitude can reduce the frequency, duration and intensity of depressive episodes. This is because giving gratitude (which is itself giving—giving thanks) re-directs their attention away from themselves.

When they look for ways to say thank you instead of indulging what may be their more natural impulse to complain, they break down the anger, frustration and resentment

HOPEfully into small chunks! This way can develop empathy and compassion.

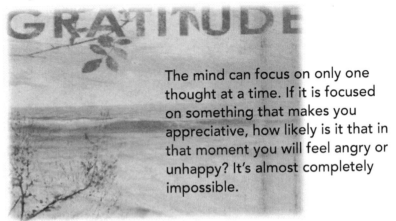

The mind can focus on only one thought at a time. If it is focused on something that makes you appreciative, how likely is it that in that moment you will feel angry or unhappy? It's almost completely impossible.

Gratitude is not simply a matter of looking at events through rose-colored glasses. Our efforts (and in some instances, fears) dictate what is important, and whether or not we unconsciously dismiss or consciously accept something. Our focus becomes our experience – reality and we decide what is rational thinking.

My review of the literature on dyslexia indicates that the research is definitive: **appreciation creates happiness**.

Mothers already have everything that they need to be happy. If they choose not to focus on the positive, they can't derive any happiness from it. To become a more grateful, joyful and peaceful person, shift your attention to what you do have, rather than to what you don't.

The adage, "You don't appreciate what you have until you lose it" is more than just a quaint saying. It is a psychological truism. When you lose something of value, your focus shifts to it, and you are reminded of the joy that it once brought.

If your attention is not on what is missing and what isn't good, then you can be surrounded by all the good fortune, blessings and material things in the world, and find happiness.

If focus creates thoughts, then thoughts create emotions. If mothers can focus on the positive, they will be a person who is filled with joy and gratitude.

Taking action, however small, can get you, your thoughts and emotions back on a healthy track.

If you focus on the negative, then you will become a person who is unhappy and unpleasant. It comes down to a choice. Are you going to live a life of appreciation or expectation? **You have a choice.**

Dr. O'Leary's Prescription:
- Cut yourself some slack today.
- Every time you feel that you can't possibly go on — you will. You've done it before and you can do it again.
- Breathe.
- Give yourself peace. You weren't called to never fail.
- Believe in yourself.
- They were born this way and there can be great HOPE for their future. Believe this for yourself and instill it in your child.

> "For I know the plans I have for you,
> plans to prosper you and not to harm you,
> plans to give you hope and a future."
> Declares the Lord.
> —Jeremiah 29:11

Thank you for being my heart's first home.
I love you, Mom.
—Maggie Lindley

COLLABORATION

The importance of a collaborative support network for the child, which includes the parents/caregiver, peers, teachers and schools working together to help them overcome difficulties, is critical.

Students with dyslexia will continue to struggle in an education system that has largely adopted a "wait and fail" approach. Support groups can help mothers ensure that their child will keep up academically with peers.

These groups can also teach your child how to recognize and avoid a range of embarrassing situations in the classroom. This may also help those who are experiencing a wide range of negative emotions that could leave lifelong scars. Good support groups will definitely help both you and your child.

It is possible that many children with dyslexia may show signs of mild autism (Asperger's), ADD and social anxiety. These children are often very good at hiding their condition, making it harder for mothers to **understand** and diagnose. If you **understand** and are aware of the components of dyslexia, you will be more aware and prepared.

Traditional teaching methods often do not work for children that are diagnosed with these conditions. Although they can be helped with *specialized* approaches, effectiveness will vary depending on the severity of the conditions and the support systems available to you.

REMEMBER
One way to think of dyslexia with mild autism (Asperger's) in a simplistic, non-scientific way would be to say that the child lacks the normal "filters" the brain uses to shut out a portion of the deluge of stimuli continually bombarding them from the outside world.

This lack of ability to filter, or **understand** stimuli can cause your child to appear totally overwhelmed by unseen stimuli. Therefore, your child may be forced to withdraw into their own private world with little ability to function on a social level.

Children with dyslexia, and sometimes Asperger's autism, have been described as having trouble with responsiveness and difficulty interacting with people and the outside world. You need to aware of the possibility of underlying co-illness.

I believe it is very important to recognize and **understand** what defines "boundaries" for a child with dyslexia. Social and emotional learning represents an important part of the foundation on which the building blocks for the needs of children with dyslexia are built. You will have to be patient, but success can be achieved.

> According to contemporary theory, dyslexia may fall somewhere in the middle of the autism spectrum. At one end, a more affected child and at the other end the mildly dyslexic child.

Support networks are vital to mothers with a dyslexic child, especially when they are young. Moms are usually the only source of that support.

Unfortunately, parents are often under enormous stress themselves in their efforts to be supportive.

Many authors and teachers have suggested that stress in parents can result from the perception that they will cause harm to their child in some way because of their lack of ability to parent their child.

SUCCESS

I have observed that a child with dyslexia can often benefit more from a sympathetic and knowledgeable counselor, than they can from academic achievements.

—Dr. O'Leary

Those who don't make good grades may be likely to give up, unless they have a caring person to help them along emotionally. Lack of success will lead them to pretend that literacy doesn't matter. Perhaps they will move into a variety of unsuitable jobs and possibly even take to crime. Some may leave school with minimal qualifications, drifting from job to job until they stumble upon one where a high degree of literacy is not an essential requirement.

There is an alarming susceptibility to drug addiction, street drugs, anxiety, depression and deep anger.

Be on guard and remind your child that you will always be there for them and love them. Talk to your child about these risks before anything happens.

> Behind every young child who believes in
> himself is a parent who believed first.
> —Mathew L. Jacobson

STORY OF THE LOVING MOTHER WHO LOST HERSELF

You matter.
- I see you wiping the tears from your child's eyes, while secretly wiping away your own.
- I see you going to an endless array of specialists and therapist visits.
- I see you struggling to keep your child calm, content and occupied in the waiting room. HOPEFUL for some good news at this appointment.

Your efforts are worth it.
- I see you searching for options all night long.
- I see your list of new things to try.

• •

I see you asking other mothers how their child was able to reach higher milestones than your own.

I see that you haven't slept or maybe even showered longer than you'd care to reveal.

I see that you haven't bought or done something for yourself in months.

I see your exhaustion.

I see your love.

Don't stop.

Persistence and determination are omnipotent.

I see you calming the meltdown.

I see you implementing the strategies you learned because you'll do anything to make this better for your child.

I see that you don't even know who you used to be before this role began.

I see you with no true close friendships.

Other people see you.

I think I know what you are going through.

I see your sadness wrapped up in a HOPEFUL smile sitting in the therapy waiting room.

I see your heart melt when your child gives you a sweet look in the midst of the chaos.

I see you waking up to do it all over again the next day.

I see your beauty and your value.

I see you not giving up no matter how hard it gets.

I see the courage and determination in you that are stronger than the disappointments and setbacks.

I see you.
And, I see me in you, and I see your HOPE.
—Ben Foss

• •

MOM...

*I want you to be encouraged by the realization
that one day, you'll look back and you will see
that you taught your child patience and perseverance.*

*You taught them unconditional love, the value of
HOPE and acceptance by not giving up.*

*You taught them it's okay to not be perfect -
that messing up and trying again is human.*

*You remind yourself that one day, when you see
the effects of sticking with it,
you'll be thankful you did.*

A MOM'S HUG
LASTS LONG AFTER
SHE LET'S GO.

FUTURE

. . . .

"As Moms, we are in it together – raising the
future. We are a tribe of future makers. So,
let's support each other."

—Marissa Hermer

RESEARCH PROGRESS

Despite a barrage of anecdotal evidence from teachers and practitioners, there is a lack of published research in self-concept and self-esteem in children with dyslexia.

One of the most exciting research discoveries in educational psychology in recent times has been the finding that student's levels of achievement are influenced by how they feel about themselves (and vice versa).

In my opinion, the limited research that has been devoted to such questions has produced some encouraging results. There is good news – self-esteem will not necessarily suffer permanently because of struggling at school. Early recognition, intervention and emotional support will help.

The fear response can create permanent memories that shape the perception of and response to a person's whole environment. Without appropriate intervention, these negative interchanges and the emotions that accompany them stack up, backing your child further and further into a corner.

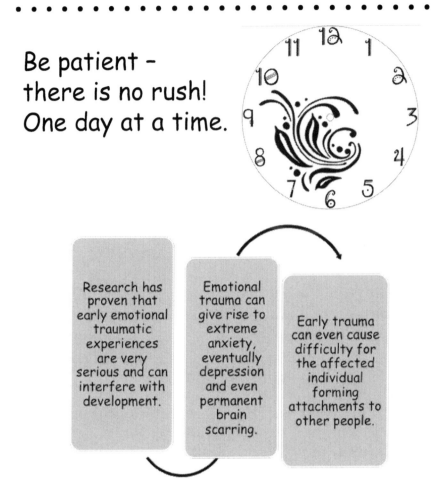

Be patient –
there is no rush!
One day at a time.

Research has proven that early emotional traumatic experiences are very serious and can interfere with development.

Emotional trauma can give rise to extreme anxiety, eventually depression and even permanent brain scarring.

Early trauma can even cause difficulty for the affected individual forming attachments to other people.

Several relevant points are fascinating. Researchers found that the same genetic factors missing in the gene for autism are also missing in the gene for dyslexia. Some researchers have concluded that there is a relationship between dyslexia and mild to moderate autism (Asperger's). Both conditions are genetic conditions that affect how your child's brain is wired.

These unusual visual effects may lead to new neurological research that is very promising. This may also lead to treatments that help retrain the brain to improve your child with dyslexia's ability to learn to read.

Despite this research on the apparent genetic basis for these conditions, it does not guarantee that both or either will manifest, but may simply note a higher probability.

Certainly, environmental factors play a role. Although both conditions exist at birth, autism may be "regressive" while dyslexia is generally not diagnosed until the child is in school learning to read.

The commonality between the two conditions, genetics and environmental, can appear on a spectrum which deals with communication interference with symbols or pictures and are processes occurring at the neuron level of the brain.

According to research, the specific cause of dyslexia is still unclear despite many symptoms that can describe both the similarities and the differences. In the case of MRI studies, the problems with processing moving images and connecting them with the sounds of letters or words is seen. But as it occurs on a spectrum, parents and teachers often confuse dyslexia with ADHD, laziness, being unmotivated or being slow.

Many times, teachers see children with dyslexia and ADD as being smart, but hard to handle due to their "attention deficit." Children with dyslexia and ADD may be thought of as lacking a few "filters." They just become easily distracted and have problems controlling their behavior.

For your child in school, everything may seem to be constantly moving or disorganized: words, letters, musical notes, numbers, even keys on a keyboard. **Your child may often say they feel overwhelmed by everything going on around them.**

A change in society is needed, especially in schools, so that failure or struggling to achieve is seen as an important part of success.

All children with dyslexia need to experience some school failure in order to, at some point, develop resilience. The key is to figure out how much failure is healthy. This is a difficult task, especially for mothers.

Over-protectiveness can hurt. Children with dyslexia need some freedom.

Overprotectiveness is another danger that many parents of dyslexic children face. Very little has been written about the danger of overprotectiveness in the parenting and advocacy literature, but it is of great concern!

In an attempt to suppress feelings of personal guilt and external blame, many mothers become overprotective. Unable to keep their child from the difficult condition, they attempt to protect them from other difficult or challenging areas of life.

> Maternal controlling can adversely affect a child with dyslexia. Be careful, stay observant and be balanced.

Do NOT become a helicopter mom. Developing into an overprotective parent, fueled by pity and guilt, may be the biggest mistake that any mother can make. Overprotective parents unwittingly create chronic dependency and "learned helplessness". This is a mindset that may persist throughout the child's life.

Key Points

- There are no obvious distinct or diagnostic neurological signs for abnormalities or brain differences with dyslexia.

- There is NO consistent evidence for cellular or tissue abnormality.

- We all have brains weighing three to three and one-half pounds. Each brain contains 100 to 200 billion cells with 75 TRILLION connections!

- Dyslexic brains are best viewed as one of many individual differences and variations. Nothing is damaged or diseased – just a connection pattern.

- Any differences in dyslexia are from circuit variation.

> Untreated ADHD can have devastating consequences in a child with dyslexia.
> —chadd.org

NEUROPLASTICITY

Research of the brain has proven that our most complex organ has the ability to rewire itself in response to experience. For many years, conventional thinking likened the mind to a steam kettle, in which pressure would build until the lid blew off. Because of this, psychologists thus encouraged people to release this buildup of pressure by venting their anger in a socially acceptable manner.

Yet after *extensive research* on the subject, it turns out that expressing anger is not only unproductive, but also destructive. When people vent their feelings aggressively, they often feel worse, increase their blood pressure and make themselves even angrier.

Scientists have even theorized that the anatomical structure of neural connections forms the basis for how children identify letters and recognize words. In other words, the brain's architecture may *predetermine* who will have trouble with reading, including children with dyslexia.

> Neuroplasticity can help moms to be more optimistic! It's really very reassuring. During the early years the brain develops the forming neural connections that pave the way for how a child will express feelings, embark on a task and learn new skills and concepts.

BUT THERE IS HOPE!!

*The idea and basis for Neuroplasticity is one great reason to have **HOPE**. A new 2018 University of Washington study has contributed greatly to our **understanding**.*

Using MRI measurements of the brain's neural connections or "white matter", these researchers have shown that in struggling readers, the neural circuitry can be strengthened.

Their reading performance can be improved after just eight weeks of a specialized tutoring program. The study, published June 8, 2018 in *Nature Communications* is the first to measure white matter during an intensive educational intervention. It links children's learning with their brains' flexibility.

It has been shown through MRI that the brain changes through the process of educating your child. These researchers were able to detect changes in brain connections within just a few weeks of beginning the intervention program.

It's underappreciated that mothers and teachers are brain engineers who help children build new brain circuits for important academic skills like reading. This study showed evidence of structural changes. The brain changes in response to proper teaching.

The children who took part in the tutoring program improved their reading skills by an average of ONE FULL GRADE LEVEL!

This experiment underscores the importance of these findings:
- The beauty of educational interventions is that they provide a means to study fundamental questions about the link between childhood experiences, brain plasticity and learning, all while giving children extra help in reading.

• •

These findings can extend to schools. Mothers and teachers have the potential to develop their children and their students' brains, regardless of whether they have the resources to provide individualized instruction for each student in their class.

While many parents and teachers might worry that dyslexia is permanent, reflecting intrinsic deficits in the brain, these findings demonstrate that targeted, intensive reading programs not only lead to substantial improvements in reading skills, but also change the underlying wiring of the brain's reading circuitry.

Whatever is repeated strengthens the neural connections, whether it is practicing a musical instrument, becoming angry or remaining calm. Every brain cell (neuron) adapts to its surroundings, more precisely, to the signals the neuron receives from neighboring cells.

When two neurons fire repeatedly at the same time, this reinforces the connection between them. Hence, the common idiom in biology: Neurons that fire together wire together. In fact, this proves true for both emotional and physical responses to stimuli.

ADHD/ADD IN CHILDREN WITH DYSLEXIA
What You Need to Know

Dyslexia and ADHD frequently coexist. Children with dyslexia often have a hard time with emotions in general. They tend to get stuck in their feelings. So, if a situation made them nervous a week ago, they may still be carrying it around with them. They also may be worried well in advance about something that will happen in the future. Think anxiety.

In my experience, using medication to help your child with ADD often improves focus and reading skills. It can help them become less irritable and better able to manage their emotions. Medication doesn't help everyone. Results of medication are apparent soon after initiation.

It is NOT addictive.

Dyslexia and ADHD are linked to other mental health issues such as anxiety, which can also drive angry reactions. These include oppositional defiance disorder (ODD) and depression. It's important to talk to your child's tutor, school or doctor about potential coexisting mental health problems which may be caused by connection problems. They frequently occur together and maybe difficult to separate.

If a child also has some ADHD, they may have frequent episodes of anger. **Temper flare-ups are common with the addition of ADHD.**

These episodes may be unpleasant and can have lingering consequences. Some teachers estimate 40% to 60% of children with dyslexia can have ADHD.

It's very common for a child with dyslexia to struggle with ADHD and even auditory processing disorders.

Those with mild **ADHD** may have problems with impulsivity or expressing emotions.

Noticing the triggers is a good first step to helping manage anger.

REMEMBER

Children often find themselves in stressful situations created by their attention issues—they may be highly sensitive and vulnerable. They may also have a hard time expressing their emotions. Because of this, if they have an angry outburst, they may feel bad about it long after everyone else has moved on.

Almost all children with dyslexia have other issues, better known as **co-morbidities**. Mothers must be very observant and **understand** the importance of these other disorders and their frequency.

Mix impulsivity with anger, and you often get an explosion. Whereas other children might quietly fume, some children might slam a door or kick the furniture. They are just not able to contain these intense feelings. **Understanding and patience** is critical at this junction.

Parents must keep their own temper and follow a few critical steps that can help their child with dyslexia and ADHD to keep theirs.

1. Take hold of your emotions. Pause long enough to think.
2. Reflect on your options and other ways you might handle yourself.

Your child needs to learn how to have self-control. Self-control involves executive function. Trouble with executive functioning, ADHD and dyslexia often go hand in hand and are often *NOT* recognized. Once again **understanding** is critical and it strongly reinforces the benefits of **HOPE**.

Imagine a day that goes like this:
Your child arrives at school without their homework and the teacher wants to know why. Later, they can't remember the directions for their worksheet, so they can't complete it. At lunch, they get teased by some kids they don't know. And during the last period of the day, they get called out for distracting a classmate. Now they come home and face more tasks, which means more things that might go wrong. They already had a stressful day, but you don't know that. You send them to make the bed they forgot to make that morning. Instead of taking it in stride, they become overwhelmed and erupt in anger.

Children who struggle with self-control and poor social skills need to be taught to stop and think. They need to think about how their anger affects other people. They can use that insight to keep their anger in check, or to stop an outburst before it's started. But this requires awareness, acceptance, **understanding** and a great deal of time and patience.

Children with dyslexia and ADHD aren't always able to use **understanding** as a way to regulate their behavior. That doesn't mean they are inconsiderate or rude. It also doesn't mean they don't feel badly about losing their temper.

In fact, once your child calms down and takes a moment to reflect, those with dyslexia and ADHD often feel terrible about how they made others feel. These negative feelings can build up and have an impact on their self-esteem. They usually are not aware of their feelings.

HOPE DOES EXIST!

- I.D.E.A. (Individuals with Disabilities Education Act) a learning disability cannot be cured or fixed; its a lifelong challenge. With appropriate support and intervention, people with learning disabilities can achieve success in school, at work, in relationships and in the community.

- Under federal law, under the (IDEA), the term is "specific learning disability," one of 13 categories of disability under that law.

- "Learning Disabilities" is an umbrella term describing a number of other, more specific learning disabilities, such as dyslexia and dysgraphia.

- I.D.A. is the International Dyslexia Association. Best in USA. Be sure to go to one. It is great!!

- IDEAS – Impacting Dyslexia Education Awareness and Support – a nonprofit organization. *http://www.ideas-plano.org/*

- Learning Disabilities Association of America. Learn more at *https://buff.ly/s2ybB9QO.org*, #LDAWorksForYou, #LearningDisibilities.com, www.LDAAmerica.org

WORK-AROUNDS

. . . .

✓ Chew gum in order to concentrate. It causes increased blood flow and provides some carbs to the brain.

✓ Don't force food– let the child determine what their taste buds prefer.

✓ Sleep – start lavender plug-ins 20-30 minutes before retiring.

✓ Pushing a dyslexic – not a good idea. There is no rush in life.

✓ Some smells can change mood; apple pie, hot chocolate, rosemary aroma.

✓ Having coffee before going to school increases brain blood flow.

✓ Lots and lots of water improves blood flow! Water bottles are essential.

✓ Mid-morning and afternoon snacks are necessary.

✓ Lists are very important!

✓ It's not imperative to make your bed in the morning.

✓ Dyslexics love sameness, consistency, predictability.

- ✓ Patriotic, fun or upbeat songs on the way to school are an effective distraction and relaxing.

- ✓ Dyslexics are fragile and vulnerable. Handle with care.

- ✓ Rejection and anger cause emotional brain scarring.

- ✓ Shower in the evening before going to bed. Never use hot water because it stimulates too many nerve endings.

- ✓ Don't force activities you like on the kids just because you may like them. Allow them to make their own choices.

- ✓ Respect and understand their senses (touch, taste, smell, sound and light). They have different ones than you.

- ✓ Repetitive movements are soothing, so let the children do them. Tapping toes, etc. are called stimming and is reassuring.

- ✓ Splashing cold water on the face helps fatigue.

- ✓ Always have a Plan B and Plan C.

- ✓ Utilize sticky notes.

SUMMARY

. . . .

Always remember your child came this way. It was not their choice. Dyslexics are very hyper-sensitive, vulnerable and hurt by rejection. Routines are calming. Handle them with care!

Your **understanding** represents the foundation for your success as a parent. Everything in raising your child is stressful. They live on a spectrum of issues and are like an iceberg; there is always more below the surface.

Remember, they are like an orchid and they will blossom because you are their loving gardener.

CONCLUSION

Love and understanding beget
hope and hope begets success
because YOU are their mom.

END NOTES

- This not for profit, non-academic manual is intended to assist mothers of a dyslexic child with the emotional and social aspects of raising their child.

- The brevity, visibility, simplicity and duplications are intended.

- Style and materials used as per Jane Friedman, professor Stanford University and 20 years of book publishing. Author of "How to Publish Your Book" and "The Business of being a Writer". University of Chicago. www.janefried.com

- Text formatted as per International Dyslexia Association, British Dyslexia Association, nonfiction education, self-publishing styles. www.fairusecommonground

- This is a not-for-profit production.

- This is an educational endeavor.

- Material may be reproduced without permission.

- "Quotation marks" are used to empathize important concepts, not as a direct quote.

INDEX

Made in the USA
Columbia, SC
07 February 2020